15 Days of Prayer
With Saint John of the Cross

Also in the *15 Days of Prayer* collection:

Saint Teresa of Ávila

Pierre Teilhard de Chardin

Saint Bernard

Saint Augustine

Thomas Merton

Saint Benedict

Meister Eckhart

Saint Francis de Sales

Johannes Tauler

Charles de Foucauld

Saint Thérèse of Lisieux

Saint Catherine of Siena

Saint Bernadette of Lourdes

Saint Thomas Aquinas

15 DAYS OF PRAYER
with
Saint John
of the Cross

CONSTANT TONNELIER

Translated by Victoria Hébert and Denis Sabourin

Liguori
LIGUORI, MISSOURI

Published by Liguori Publications
Liguori, Missouri
http://www.liguori.org

This book is a translation of *Prier 15 Jours Avec Jean de la Croix,*
published by Nouvelle Cité, 1990, Montrouge, France.

Library of Congress Cataloging-in-Publication Data
Tonnelier, Constant.
    [Prier 15 jours avec Jean de la Croix. English]
    15 days of prayer with Saint John of the Cross / Constant
Tonnelier ; translated by Victoria Hébert and Denis Sabourin. — 1st
English ed.
          p. cm.
    Includes bibliographical references.
    ISBN 0-7648-0654-8 (pbk.)
    1. John of the Cross, Saint, 1542–1591—Meditations. 2.
Spiritual life—Catholic Church. I. Title: Fifteen days of prayer with
Saint John of the Cross. II. Title.

BX4700.J7 T6613 2000
269'.6—dc21   00–029602

Printed in the United States of America
04 03 02 01 00   5 4 3 2 1
First English Edition 2000

Table of Contents

How to Use This Book ▪ vii

A Brief Chronology of the Life of Saint John of the Cross ▪ xv

Introduction ▪ xxi

Abbreviations Used in This Book ▪ xxiii

1. Day One—To Want to Know You in
    Order to Resemble You ▪ 1

2. Day Two—To Let Myself Be Wounded in
    Order to Find You ▪ 8

3. Day Three—Consumed With the Desire
    for Your Presence ▪ 15

4. Day Four—Wounded, Am I Totally Yours? ▪ 21

5. Day Five—Christ, to Discover Who You Are in
    Order to Be Yours ▪ 28

6. Day Six—How Can I Become Like You? ▪ 35

7. Day Seven—Going to You With All the Strength
    of My Will ▪ 41

8. Day Eight—My Path Could Only Be Yours ▪ 47

9. Day Nine—Purify My Knowledge ▪ 54

10. Day Ten—Christ, While I Am on the Path,
    You Are My Only Support ▪ 61

11. Day Eleven—In Order to Get Close to You,
    I Must Rid Myself of Everything ▪ 68

12. Day Twelve—Purified, I Rest in You ▪ 75

13. Day Thirteen—My Gaze Has Become Yours ▪ 82

14. Day Fourteen—Your Love Always Carries Me Further ▪ 89

15. Day Fifteen—Transformed by God,
    I Find My True Image Again ▪ 96

Bibliography ▪ 103

How to Use This Book

AN OLD CHINESE PROVERB, or at least what I am able to recall of what is supposed to be an old Chinese proverb, goes something like this: "Even a journey of a thousand miles begins with a single step." When you think about it, the truth of the proverb is obvious. It is impossible to begin any project, let alone a journey, without taking the first step. I think it might also be true, although I cannot recall if another Chinese proverb says it, "that the first step is often the hardest." Or, as someone else once observed, "the distance between a thought and the corresponding action needed to implement the idea takes the most energy." I don't know who shared that perception with me but I am certain it was not an old Chinese master!

With this ancient proverbial wisdom, and the not-so-ancient wisdom of an unknown contemporary sage still fresh, we move from proverbs to presumptions. How do these relate to the task before us?

I am presuming that if you are reading this introduction it is because you are contemplating a journey. My presumption is that you are preparing for a spiritual journey and that you have taken at least some of the first steps necessary to prepare for this journey. I also presume, and please excuse me if I am making too many presumptions, that in your preparation for the spiritual journey you have determined that you need a guide.

From deep within the recesses of your deepest self, there was something that called you to consider John of the Cross as a potential companion. If my presumptions are correct, may I congratulate you on this decision? I think you have made a wise choice, a choice that can be confirmed by yet another source of wisdom, the wisdom that comes from practical experience.

Even an informal poll of experienced travelers will reveal a common opinion; it is very difficult to travel alone. Some might observe that it is even foolish. Still others may be even stronger in their opinion and go so far as to insist that it is necessary to have a guide, especially when you are traveling into uncharted waters and into territory that you have not yet experienced. I am of the personal opinion that a traveling companion is welcome under all circumstances. The thought of traveling alone, to some exciting destination without someone to share the journey with does not capture my imagination or channel my enthusiasm. However, with that being noted, what is simply a matter of preference on the normal journey becomes a matter of necessity when a person embarks on a spiritual journey.

The spiritual journey, which can be the most challenging of all journeys, is experienced best with a guide, a companion, or at the very least, a friend in whom you have placed your trust. This observation is not a preference or an opinion but rather an established spiritual necessity. All of the great saints with whom I am familiar had a spiritual director or a confessor who journeyed with them. Admittedly, at times the saint might well have traveled far beyond the experience of their guide and companion but more often than not they would return to their director and reflect on their experience. Understood in this sense, the director and companion provided a valuable contribution and necessary resource.

When I was learning how to pray (a necessity for anyone who desires to be a full-time and public "religious person"), the community of men that I belong to gave me a great gift. Between my second and third year in college, I was given a one-year sabbatical, with all expenses paid and all of my personal needs met. This period of time was called novitiate. I was officially designated as a novice, a beginner in the spiritual journey, and I was assigned a "master," a person who was willing to lead me. In addition to the master, I was provided with every imaginable book and any other resource that I could possibly need. Even with all that I was provided, I did not learn how to pray because of the books and the unlimited resources, rather it was the master, the companion who was the key to the experience.

One day, after about three months of reading, of quiet and solitude, and of practicing all of the methods and descriptions of prayer that were available to me, the master called. "Put away the books, forget the method, and just listen." We went into a room, became quiet, and tried to recall the presence of God, and then, the master simply prayed out loud and permitted me to listen to his prayer. As he prayed, he revealed his hopes, his dreams, his struggles, his successes, and most of all, his relationship with God. I discovered as I listened that his prayer was deeply intimate but most of all it was self-revealing. As I learned about him, I was led through his life experience to the place where God dwells. At that moment I was able to understand a little bit about what I was supposed to do if I really wanted to pray.

The dynamic of what happened when the master called, invited me to listen, and then revealed his innermost self to me as he communicated with God in prayer, was important. It wasn't so much that the master was trying to reveal to me what needed to be said; he was not inviting me to pray with the same words that he used, but rather that he was trying to bring me to that place within myself where prayer becomes possible. That place, a place of intimacy and of self-awareness, was a necessary stop on the journey and it was a place that I needed to be led to. I could not have easily discovered it on my own.

The purpose of the volume that you hold in your hand is to lead you, over a period of fifteen days or, maybe more realistically, fifteen prayer periods, to a place where prayer is possible. If you already have a regular experience and practice of prayer, perhaps this volume can help lead you to a deeper place, a more intimate relationship with the Lord.

It is important to note that the purpose of this book is not to lead you to a better relationship with John of the Cross, your spiritual companion. Although your companion will invite you to share some of their deepest and most intimate thoughts, your companion is doing so only to bring you to that place where God dwells. After all, the true measurement of a companion for the journey is that they bring you to the place where you need to be, and then they step back, out of the picture. A guide who brings you to the desired destination and then sticks around is a very unwelcome guest!

Many times I have found myself attracted to a particular idea or method for accomplishing a task, only to discover that what seemed to be inviting and helpful possessed too many details. All of my energy went to the mastery of the details and I soon lost my enthusiasm. In each instance, the book that seemed so promising ended up on my bookshelf, gathering dust. I can assure you, it is not our intention that this book end up in your bookcase, filled with promise, but unable to deliver.

There are three simple rules that need to be followed in order to use this book with a measure of satisfaction.

Place: It is important that you choose a place for reading that provides the necessary atmosphere for reflection and that does not allow for too many distractions. Whatever place you choose needs to be comfortable, have the necessary lighting, and, finally, have a sense of "welcoming" about it. You need to be able to look forward to the experience of the journey. Don't travel steerage if you know you will be more comfortable in first class and if the choice is realistic for you. On the other hand, if first class is a distraction and you feel more comfortable and more yourself in steerage, then it is in steerage that you belong.

My favorite place is an overstuffed and comfortable chair in my bedroom. There is a light over my shoulder, and the chair reclines if I feel a need to recline. Once in a while, I get lucky and the sun comes through my window and bathes the entire room in light. I have other options and other places that are available to me but this is the place that I prefer.

Time: Choose a time during the day when you are most alert and when you are most receptive to reflection, meditation, and prayer. The time that you choose is an essential component. If you are a morning person, for example, you should choose a time that is in the morning. If you are more alert in the afternoon, choose an afternoon time slot; and if evening is your preference, then by all means choose the evening. Try to avoid "peak" periods in your daily routine when you know that you might be disturbed. The time that you choose needs to be your time and needs to work for you.

It is also important that you choose how much time you

will spend with your companion each day. For some it will be possible to set aside enough time in order to read and reflect on all the material that is offered for a given day. For others, it might not be possible to devote one time to the suggested material for the day, so the prayer period may need to be extended for two, three, or even more sessions. It is not important how long it takes you; it is only important that it works for you and that you remain committed to that which is possible.

For myself I have found that fifteen minutes in the early morning, while I am still in my robe and pajamas and before my morning coffee, and even before I prepare myself for the day, is the best time. No one expects to see me or to interact with me because I have not yet "announced" the fact that I am awake or even on the move. However, once someone hears me in the bathroom, then my window of opportunity is gone. It is therefore important to me that I use the time that I have identified when it is available to me.

Freedom: It may seem strange to suggest that freedom is the third necessary ingredient, but I have discovered that it is most important. By freedom I understand a certain "stance toward life," a "permission to be myself and to be gentle and understanding of who I am." I am constantly amazed at how the human person so easily sets himself or herself up for disappointment and perceived failure. We so easily make judgments about ourselves and our actions and our choices, and very often those judgments are negative, and not at all helpful.

For instance, what does it really matter if I have chosen a place and a time, and I have missed both the place and the time for three days in a row? What does it matter if I have chosen, in that twilight time before I am completely awake and still a little sleepy, to roll over and to sleep for fifteen minutes more? Does it mean that I am not serious about the journey, that I really don't want to pray, that I am just fooling myself when I say that my prayer time is important to me? Perhaps, but I prefer to believe that it simply means that I am tired and I just wanted a little more sleep. It doesn't mean anything more than that. However, if I make it mean more than that, then I can become discouraged, frustrated, and put myself into a state where I might more easily give up. "What's the use? I might as well forget all about it."

The same sense of freedom applies to the reading and the praying of this text. If I do not find the introduction to each day helpful, I don't need to read it. If I find the questions for reflection at the end of the appointed day repetitive, then I should choose to close the book and go my own way. Even if I discover that the reflection offered for the day is not the one that I prefer and that the one for the next day seems more inviting, then by all means, go on to the one for the next day.

That's it! If you apply these simple rules to your journey you should receive the maximum benefit and you will soon find yourself at your destination. But be prepared to be surprised. If you have never been on a spiritual journey you should know that the "travel brochures" and the other descriptions that you might have heard are nothing compared to the real thing. There is so much more than you can imagine.

A final prayer of blessing suggests itself:

Lord, catch me off guard today.
Surprise me with some moment of beauty
  or pain
So that at least for the moment
I may be startled into seeing that you are
  here in all your splendor,
Always and everywhere,
Barely hidden,
Beneath,
Beyond,
Within this life I breathe.

Frederick Buechner

REV. THOMAS M. SANTA, CSsR
LIGUORI, MISSOURI
FEAST OF THE PRESENTATION, 1999

A Brief Chronology of the Life of Saint John of the Cross

JOHN OF THE CROSS, although not a prolific writer, was
one to seize the opportunity to communicate with his readers
as a mystic, poet, teacher, and ardent lover of God. His works
do not compare in quantity and thematic variety with the writings of other Doctors of the Church, but he did leave us four
major works of prose: *The Ascent of Mount Carmel*; *The Dark
Night of the Soul*; *The Spiritual Canticles*; and *The Living Flame
of Love*. The only other writings that were left are a few scarce
letters and counsels. In his writings, he dwells on the following main themes, which are constant: union with God—
Trinitarian origins and glorious outcome; Jesus Christ—the
Word and the Beloved; faith—as part of the mystery and the
way to the union; love—the exit from one's self to live in the
other; the active and passive development of the spiritual life;
communication with God through silent prayer; the human
appetites for sin and self-destruction.

John of the Cross holds an important place in Spanish lit-
erature for his poetry; yet his prose style is less conventional—
sometimes using common images, other times using concepts,
theological terms, and biblical symbols—a style that is uniquely
his own—often complex, repetitive, and cluttered, very dis-

concerting to the reader. It is interesting to note that his original transcripts have all been lost—his writings come to us through numerous codices.

John of the Cross was an influential contemporary, friend, and co-founder, with Teresa of Ávila, of the Discalced Friars. The Bible served as his hymnal, his companion, and book of meditation—his one source of the living waters of the Word. The following will give the reader a sketch of his life as it unfolded:

1542: Juan de Yepes was born on June 24 in Fontiveros, Spain; the son of Gonzalo de Yepes and Catalina Alvarez. He was the third of three sons. His father was of the nobility (silk merchant) who sacrificed his social standing and wealth in order to marry Catalina (a poor silk weaver).

1545–1558:
 Gonzalo died in 1545; some say it was as a result of being forced to adapt to the rigors of poverty and hard work. Catalina traveled to Toledo to seek help from her late husband's family—she was rejected and returned home.

 In 1547, Luis, the second son died.

 In 1551, the family moved to Medina del Campo and John began to receive his elementary education at a school for poor children where he was also fed and clothed. He tried various apprenticeships (1551–8) and served as an acolyte at La Magdalena.

1559: John found work, at the age of seventeen, at the Medina hospital and enrolled in the Jesuit College, where he studied the humanities and philosophy.

1563–1568:
 John entered the Carmelite Order in Medina (Santa Ana) in 1563 and changed his name to Fray Juan de Santo Malia; he professed his vows the following year.

From 1564–8, he attended the University of Salamanca in a three-year arts program, followed by one year of theological studies. He was elected prefect of studies during this time which attested to his talents and intelligence (he taught classes and assisted the regent master).

In 1567, he was ordained and met Teresa of Ávila when he was saying his first Mass in Medina. She spoke to him of her plans to restore the Carmelite Primitive Rule for both the friars and the nuns. John, who often thought of transferring to the Carthusians because he sought a more contemplative life, promised Teresa he would adopt her reformed life. He traveled to Valladolid with Teresa to spend a few months learning the Teresian way of life.

On November 28, 1568, he professed the Carmelite Primitive Rule, changing his name to Fray John of the Cross. He was appointed subprior and novice master of their first house in Duruelo. This life would be one of hardship and contemplation, but the friars also actively preached and heard confessions. It is interesting to note that the friars adopted the habit of wearing sandals on their feet and, from this time onward, were referred to as the Discalced Carmelites. Their habits were of dark brown coarse cloth, often thought to be made of goat hair, with a white cloak. John may have been tonsured.

1570–1578:

In 1570, John moved his community to Mancera de Abajo due to the unhealthy conditions in Duruelo.

In 1571, he accompanied Teresa to Alba for her foundation there; he was named rector of the university college of Alcala de Henares.

In May of 1572, at the request of Teresa of Ávila, Fray John became the vicar and confessor of the monastery at Incarnation—he would remain there (with a few brief interruptions) until 1577.

In 1574 and 1575, he accompanied Teresa on various foundations.

In January of 1576, Fray John was arrested, for the first time, by the Carmelites of the Observance (who opposed the reforms)—he was released through the intervention of the nuncio. He was unable to offer much physical resistance as he was very small of stature—measuring just four feet eleven inches.

After the death of the nuncio in 1577, John was abducted in Ávila, brought to Toledo, and imprisoned for nine months in the monastery prison for refusing to renounce the reform. It was during this time that he composed some of his greatest works; *The Spiritual Canticles* and *The Dark Night of the Soul* were written at this time. In August, he made a miraculous escape from prison by "picking" the lock of his cell, slipping past a guard, and climbing out of a window using a rope made of strips of blankets. Taking only his book of writings, not knowing where he was, he followed a dog to civilization in Toledo, hiding in a convent infirmary where he read his poems to the nuns.

In November, a secret chapter of the Discalced Carmelites was held.

1579–1589:

Many foundations were made and Fray John did a great deal of administrating and writing. His mother died in 1580 and the pope (Gregory XIII) decreed a separation between the Calced and Discalced Carmelites which was put into action in 1581 when John was named definitor. He traveled to Ávila to bring Teresa back to make more foundations, but this was impossible due to her ill health. He recruited Ana de Jesus as co-founder in her place. *The Ascent of Mount Carmel* was written in the period 1581–5.

In 1582, John became prior at Granada; October 4th saw the death of Teresa of Ávila.

1583–1588 saw John involved in various foundations and much reform from within the ranks. In 1585, *The Living Flame of Love* was written.

In 1588, he was elected first councilor in the new form of government called the consulata and took up residence in Segovia; he often acted as major definitor and president of the consulata.

In 1589, as prior of Segovia, he built a new monastery.

1590–1591:

The chapter meetings in 1590 and 1591 were stormy, with many serious disagreements surfacing regarding the desired abandonment (by Father Doria) of jurisdiction over the nuns founded by Teresa. John opposed Doria and, as a result, John was not appointed to any office and he offered to travel to Mexico (June 1591); he retired to Andalusia, suffering from fevers and gangrenous sores on his foot (some sources say it was his leg). He moved to Ubeda ("where he wasn't known") where he begrudgingly sought medical help, as he did not like to sacrifice his love of solitude. This was not met with favor by the prior there who was concerned with the added expense of it all. By December of that year, John's condition had worsened; on December 11th, John asked for Viaticum; on December 13th, he bade farewell and asked for the prior's forgiveness for any problems he may have caused; last rites were administered and John of the Cross died, as he had predicted, as the clock struck midnight (so he could sing matins in heaven), with the following words on his lips: "Into your hands, O Lord, I commend my spirit."

In either 1592 or 1593, his remains were transferred to Segovia. He was beatified by Clement X in 1675, canonized by Benedict XIII in 1726, and declared a Doctor of the Church by Pius XI in 1926. In 1952, the Spanish Ministry of National Education named John of the Cross the patron saint of Spanish poets. His feast day is December 14th (formerly November 24th). He is called the Doctor of Mystical Theology.

The major events of John of the Cross's life don't give us a full picture of his character and personal spirituality. His early "firsthand" experiences with poverty and deprivation, coupled with his later misunderstandings, imprisonment, and persecution, might have caused him to become a bitter cynic; but instead, the result was a man who was purified and enlightened with a clear vision of the beauty of God's creation and an intimacy with the Blessed Trinity.

Introduction

TO HAVE PURCHASED and opened the cover of this book is already a sign of a call that echoed in the depth of your heart. You have heard the words of the Father and felt that they were falling on you like they did on his only Son: "You are the child of my love." It is a call to make your life as a child of God grow so that you can live, turned towards the Father, and become able, in him, to unite, in the same glance of love, the Lord, your brothers and sisters, and your daily life.

The comments offered in this book will be an enlightenment for each of us to enter into the thoughts of the guide and, through that, join with God. But we must always return to the words of the master by becoming his disciples. It will also be necessary to designate an amount of time for both the Lord and us. Intimacy can only be built in silence; it always calls for a certain quiet, a total presence to the other, an availability of heart and being. Courage will be necessary, and so will steadfastness. But the Lord will be there because he has called us to the meeting. And who could want us to reach a "resemblance," if not the one who made us "children of his love"? Then, very simply, let us get onto the path. Saint John of the Cross will lead us in the discovery of the depths and the summits which enlighten, with a new light and a new meaning, our daily lives which are, at times, so covered in darkness.

John of the Cross invites us *"to strip ourselves of everything that is not God, for God. Let us love in truth, our heart is no longer our own."* The entire task consists of dwelling before our God, *"detached, stripped, pure and simple, with no way or manner of being."* Then, God will come to take all of the space that is free in us and fill us with his love.

Let us mark out the path so we can progress all the way to the union of resemblance with the Lord Jesus. Let us go ahead all the way, allowing ourselves to be freed by you, Jesus.

There are four major stages:

1. Man who found the desire for God—he continues to seek him; he is wounded; he wants to unite himself with God.
2. What does it mean to be united with God?—Is it not to let oneself be transformed by him all the way to the union of our will to his own will?
3. For that to happen, purification is necessary—in the very depths of our being: our will, intelligence, memory.
4. In this way, we let ourselves be transformed in God—purified, we are free to love; we love with God's love; with a love that is always in movement, progressing, all the way until we find our true image, at the very heart of the Trinity.

Here are descriptions of these propositions for reflection for these fifteen days of silence and meetings with the Lord. With reference to the titles of each chapter—each is "a lead wire." Each title explains the profound content of the thought of Saint John of the Cross and the commentator. It is useful, then, to return to them, at one time or another, during the course of our prayers. If they make up a part of our memory, then they will also inhabit our hearts.

Abbreviations Used
in This Book

ED   Various Writings

MC II, 5; 3   *The Ascent of Mount Carmel*, book 2, chapter 5;
            paragraph 3

NO II, 24; 4 *The Dark Night of the Soul*, book 2, chapter 24;
            paragraph 4

CS 5; 4, 6   *The Spiritual Canticles*, stanza 5; paragraphs 4 and 6

VF 1; 12   *The Living Flame of Love*, stanza 1; paragraph 12

DAY ONE

To Want to Know You in Order to Resemble You

FOCUS POINT

We are created in God's image, the beauty of the Lord is apparent in every one of us. We can come to know God the Father, the Son, and Holy Spirit better through prayer, and allow the Holy Trinity to transform us from within so that we resemble the love of God more fully. To seek God is to know God; to seek him out in every corner of our lives, find him in all things. This is our daily challenge.

Dripping with a thousand graces,
hastily, he crossed our woods.
In his travels, he looked at them.
His face, which was etched there
is enough to leave them clothed with beauty.

"He (the Son of God) is the reflection of God's glory and the exact imprint of God's very being..." (Heb 1:3).

It must be known, then, that God looked at all things through this image of His Son alone, which gave them their natural state of being, their beauty, and their many natural gifts and graces which made them complete and perfect, even as He says in Genesis: "God saw everything that he had made, and, indeed, it was very good..." (1:31).

He exalted man in the beauty of God, and, consequently, through man, exalted all creatures, because by uniting Himself with man, He united Himself with all the creatures had by their common nature with Him... (CS 5:4).

Wounded with love by this trace of the beauty of its Beloved that it perceives in creatures, the soul, with the desire to contemplate this invisible beauty that has created a visible beauty in it, proclaims:

Ah, who will be able to heal me!
Surrender yourself completely!

The more that the soul knows God, the more it is consumed with desire to see Him. And when it sees that there is nothing that can cure its pain except the sight and the presence of its Beloved, it wants no other remedy. It begs Him to make it fully enjoy His presence.... Only the sight of Him can satisfy the love it has for Him. It then beseeches Him to surrender Himself to it fully in complete and perfect love: Surrender yourself completely!

To know God in His essence is the true knowledge that the soul seeks.

My Lord and my Spouse, give me completely what, up until now, You have only partially given to me. What You have only given me glimpses of, show me now in its full light....

Give Yourself in truth, give Yourself completely to my whole soul... (CS 6:1, 2, 5).

<hr>

T here are many ways to look at this world in which we live. The various media capture the "happening" stories, seeking the sensational. Often, they grasp onto that which is evil and that which produces evil. But what about the good, where is it? Certain people, with pessimistic tendencies, no longer know how to discern for themselves what is of value or seems to be of value. In our world, the good often is mixed in with that which is evil. That is evident. But we can change the way we look at things and learn to look at them as God does and with God. In a single glance, he encompasses beings as well as things, detecting either the initial beauty of the Creation or the beauty that was restored by the Son in them. *There was day and night and God saw that it was good* (see Gen 1).

The Supreme Beauty could only create beauty. In this cosmos, everything is in equilibrium and a simple reflection of the creative Beauty. What glimpses could the Beautiful One discover? The glimpses that include Man and Woman, *created in God's image*, into whom God *breathed his breath of life* (Gen 1), who were able to marvel at each other in a face-to-face which led to the creative glance that made the other's existence possible. That is the primordial work of God, his first gaze of love: *He exalted man in the beauty of God, and, consequently, through man, exalted all creatures*, done for him as he had something in common with this Universe. A creation that was dripping with a thousand graces. However, a seductive glance leads to a destructive glance. The human glance is tarnished, yet God's glance remains transparent. But how can we bring this to Man? Through the Only Son, "the reflection of God's glory and the exact imprint of God's very being" (Heb 1:3). "And the Word became flesh and lived among us, and we have seen his glory, the glory as a father's only son, full of grace and truth.... No one has ever seen God. It is God the only Son, who is close to the Father's heart, who has made him known" (Jn 1:14, 18).

Jesus, through his human face, reflected his inner beauty at the same time as he expressed the perfect equilibrium of his human nature. He shone with the charm of all creatures to the point that all came to him. He appropriated nothing for himself, but freed each person from whatever had bound them. His glance penetrated all the way to the deepest depths, so that each person could envisage a new future. To cross his glance called for a transformation of the human glance, making it able to contemplate God, the Supreme Beauty, God in his Glory. It was the glance of an Only Son for his Father. It was a glance of the Father for the Son of his love.

This is a personal step for us to experience for our own. Which glances are our own? Are they glances of appropriation, destruction, seduction, incomprehension, or reproach? Perhaps we must begin by plunging our glances into those of the Son so that we can see in a different way. Perhaps we must allow the intense desire to know the Son grow within us so that we resemble him. Perhaps we must recognize all of our various "blind spots" by agreeing to offer ourselves to the lightning-like light of Christ. But it takes time to adapt or re-adapt to God.

Let us utter Moses' prayer: "he persevered as though he saw him who was invisible" (Heb 11:27); "show me your glory, I pray" (Ex 33:18). And the Lord answered: "I will make all my goodness pass before you, and will proclaim before you the name, 'The Lord'; and I will be gracious to whom I will be gracious, and will show mercy on whom I will show mercy" (Ex 33:19).

For every being, hence each one of us, there always exists traces of the Beauty of the Lord. Cry out to God, call upon the mercy of God who is pleased to be gracious, so that beyond that which is visible, even disfigured, we can reach all of the way to the Invisible One. But may this transfigured invisibility lead us to the contemplation of the invisible Beauty? Not to dream or imagine it, but very simply to discover, through the thousands of graces of beauty, the reflections of the One who is all-Beauty. We must return everything to Him, as we are penetrated by his presence and his glance, healed from seeing that which is only on the surface, so that everything happens in the depths of our being, within that which dwells in our will and heart.

Lord, surrender yourself completely! It is true that your gifts are many, but I am finite. Bring your work in me to a good end, Lord, by never ceasing to surrender yourself to me. But also, give me a thirst for you; make the desire in my heart for you come alive again.

To glance at you leads me to know you, the One who spoke to us through your Son, the Word, the Word made Flesh. He is the Word that stakes out the road of life. It is a Word of hope and a call. It is a Word that rectifies and transforms. It is a Word that marvels and conquers all the way to a loving response. It is a Word that never ceases to echo in the heart which welcomes it until it fascinates in the new world. It is a Word, then, that becomes our own when the living Love of God will have led us into his own love for all time, that is to say, in him and in his life.

But the road unfolds its path in our human life today. It is here, now, that we must deepen our knowledge of God, through a prayer of contemplation and a filial face-to-face with God, thanks to the Church to whom Jesus entrusted the ministry of the Word, thanks to the witnesses who travel the same road as we do, and thanks to the Book of Scriptures that has been placed into our hands.

It is a road that comes to its end under a limitless, endless horizon, God's heaven. It is the time for the meeting and God's vision. It is the time when all of his presences on earth—in the Eucharist, in the Scriptures, in the hearts of believers, in each being that makes God his Guest—illuminate themselves in the Unique Presence of the Sovereign Beauty.

These presences in faith today lead to and develop the love that we bring to God. The intense desire of the being, one day, plunged into Love, in God's heart, delivered to Love, consumed in Love, all the way to not being able to do anything except in communion with Love. It is the time when we will see the glory, where we will recognize it as we are recognized. But then we must change our glances. It is only through Christ that we will be able to discover the traces of beauty, of the Unique Beauty, in our universe. It is only through him that the partial way that we live will find its cohesion. It is only through him that our glance will become illuminated. It is only through him that our desire to know him better will grow in order to live, like him, as a son, turned towards the Father.

REFLECTION QUESTIONS

Saint Ignatius of Loyola challenged himself to "see God in all things." Do I make an effort to see God in all people? In all situations? Do I tend to think the best of people or the worst? Do I see God in myself or do I criticize and belittle myself to the point where I cannot identify him in my life? When I see God in myself and in others am I transformed by this image, moved to pursue God in every aspect of my life?

DAY TWO

To Let Myself Be Wounded in Order to Find You

FOCUS POINT
There is a battle within us, a struggle deep inside, that causes us great pain. This agony, the fight between what is our will and what is God's will, is a wound, an opening through which God enters into our hearts. Love is a wound. When we love, something inside of us dies; something we cared about, that meant so much to us, even though it was not for our own good. God's will directs us to the greater good.

All those who we see passing by here
speak of your marvels,
but all of that only wounds me,
and leaves me to die,
they pass by mumbling something, I don't know what.

In this work of love, there are three kinds of pain which correspond to three kinds of knowledge that the soul can have of the Beloved.

The first is a simple wound, which heals quickly because it comes out of a kind of knowledge that the soul receives from the creatures, which are the lowest works of God. (...)

The second is a sore, which takes firmer hold upon the soul than the wound, and for that reason lasts longer, for it is like a wound which has become a sore. The soul that has this sore truly carries the scars of love within it. These sores come from the knowledge of the works of the Incarnation of the Word and the other mysteries of faith which are greater works of God, due to a greater love than the one that produced inferior creatures. (...)

The third kind of pain in love is like the agony of dying. The sore has festered and the inflammation spreads to the entire soul. The life of this soul is continuous agony up until the day when love, bringing its last effort to it, transforms it into love, in order to make it live a life of love. And this agony of love is caused by a sovereign touch of the Divinity, by this "something," as is said in this stanza, "that the creatures are barely able to stammer." This touch is neither continuous nor long, for were it so, the soul would break its bonds with the body. This touch passes quickly, and leaves the soul to die of love: it is an agony that will always increase for it is clear to the soul that love will not give it death. (...)

One of the great favors that God grants to souls in this life is to give them the knowledge and such a sublime taste of himself that it becomes clear to them that they could neither know or taste Him fully. This viewpoint has a certain relationship to the state of those who are blessed to see Him in heaven. There, those who know Him the best understand, even more clearly,

that there is infinitely more of Him left for them to understand
(CS 7:2–4, 9).

———

W hy must we allow ourselves to be wounded in order
to find you, Lord? You never impose yourself on man
since your respect for his freedom is so profound. You seek the
opening through which you can penetrate into his heart and
his life. Not just any opening. Not just a simple surface wound,
or even a sore which goes a little deeper. You seek the opening
of an agony, a deep inner battle which makes one die to himself and a thousand other things in order to finally live of you,
in order to allow your fiery love to invade the heart. Is not all
love in itself a wound? We only truly love if we allow the other
person to penetrate into ourselves. But this entrance of another into ourselves demands that we first take our leave of
ourselves, so that a breech is made in us, a tearing apart, a
wound which will free our heart and our whole being of all
desire for possession or self-closure in order to become available to the other and respectful of what he is.

I recognize that: "O Lord, you have enticed me, and I was
enticed; you have overpowered me, and you have prevailed. I
have become a laughingstock all day long; everyone mocks
me. For whenever I speak, I must cry out, I must shout, 'Vio-
lence and destruction!' For the word of the Lord has become
for me a reproach and derision all day long. If I say 'I will not
mention him, or speak any more in his name,' then within me
there is something like a burning fire shut up in my bones; I
am weary with holding it in, and I cannot" (Jer 20:7–9). I am
hurt by such a strong love, by the strength of your love, Lord,
how can I not open myself to such a love?

There are many ways to open oneself to it. All of creation and the universe give witness to the creative love of God. To know how to look upon these marvels by God, God's works, which are also works that have come from man's intelligence, in order to discover God presupposes a flight from one's self and the offer of a welcome to other realities. But external wounds aren't the only things that lead one to a life transformation and a vehement and consuming love. Just as profound, but in another way, is the sore caused by *"the knowledge of the works of the Incarnation of the Word and the other mysteries of faith which are greater works of God,"* the expression of the depth of the love of God the Father, manifested in his Son, Jesus. These are sores that come from the mystery of the Incarnation, a reality of our life in Christ. It is the opening of a sore in us through faith in the truth of the Incarnation: the Son of God who fully assumed his humanity in a body born of the Virgin Mary through the action of the Holy Spirit. It was a humanity that was fully submitted to the requirements of the life of a newborn, a child, and adolescent. He was not a God who lived like a God, but a God who lived human trials like each one of us, not forgetting the education, training for human life, as well as a religious life that was provided for him by Mary and Joseph. It was a humanity that was shared with a group of chosen people, the Twelve Apostles, who were as admiring of the joyous spontaneities of it as they were shocked by the incomprehension of the Mystery. It was a humanity that was profoundly wounded to its very core, from the time of the passion to the hour of his death on the cross, when everything abandoned him, when even the Father remained silent. The humanity had a body that was bruised and bloodied and a heart that was filled with the anguish that was the evil in man—sin—waiting for this heart to open itself and let the water and the blood of grace and life flow into it. The recognition of the Incarnation of the Word in its reality, the source of reality for our life in Christ through faith and grace. No, it cannot happen—not without wounds, not without sores, not without a breech in my beautiful human creations. How can I imagine this? God of love, I will only find you if I allow myself to be wounded. And the sore won't be enough. You propose to lead me all the way to agony, all the way to an inner battle which will conclude with my liberation from my self in order to live a life of love, to live of you, Lord, you who are Love, to live a life like you, Jesus, the life of one who arises from death. I must always work harder to know you, to get to know you by being with you, until this knowledge creates a love in me that carries me along and plunges me into Love. It is an agony that will lead me to the primordial choice that is you and will make me abandon the futilities as well as the serious realities of human life. It is a primordial choice like that of the merchant in the Gospel: "in search of fine pearls, on finding one pearl of great value, he went and sold all that he had and bought it" (Mt 13:45–46). It is a choice that is preceded by numerous approaches, for any deep cut is scary because it causes pain, just as hesitation, in the face of the primordial choice, is painful. It is a choice that is never without risks. The risk to be weighted down by one's humanity all the way to the remittance of one's self into the hands of God, *"when God's love, bringing its last effort to it,"* which transforms our existence, *"in order to make it live a life of love."* The agony is the passage of our multiple daily realities beyond death in order to reach Life, *"to live a life of love."* It is an agony that, at times, may be very painful, but one which leads, at an unexpected time, to the discovery of, and intense joy in, the Life of the Love of God in us. It is a pearl of great value, a precious pearl for which we renounce everything else and sacrifice it all. The only ones who discover the pearl of love are the ones who allow themselves to be interiorly wounded by the dart of God's love. The Lord is not the One who usually strikes a lightning blow. Taking into consideration our capacities to welcome what he is, he proceeds by small repeated touches: *"touches that are neither continuous nor long."* We must be open to them in order to perceive them, we must have a thirst to love and be loved. We must be seekers of God, humble and poor, in order to recognize that we can only bring our personal experience of God's love through stammerings, each experience is as unique as God's love for each of us is singular. We must let ourselves be carried by and lifted up by love, without breaking with the source from which we quench ourselves daily.

To find the source of Love, which is God, and to live his life of love, does not remove us from the preoccupations of the world, or from the weight of human toils or from the questions that are asked along the route. But if the wellspring of Love flows within us, all of humanity will take on a new meaning and the many "whys" of life will have an answer.

However, life on earth is a passage where only a few references will give us a taste of the sublimity of the Love of God and an astounding discovery of the gift of his Life. From one reference to another, the passage continues, punctuated with wounds, or sores, or agonies. And the reference is there that will give us the taste of these bountiful hours, humble glimmers of what the light of the Kingdom will be. Our knowledge will be greater and our love will be more profound. But in order to reach this point, I must allow myself to be wounded and open a breech in my heart to let love enter.

REFLECTION QUESTIONS

How do I feel when I die to something in my life in favor of the greater good, of what God would have me do? What has been the most difficult and challenging example of this in my life? What obstacles (bad habits, harmful relationships I will not leave) remain in my life that sometimes take precedence over what God would have me do? What steps might I take to overcome these obstacles and unite my will with that of God?

DAY THREE

Consumed With the Desire for Your Presence

FOCUS POINT

The desire to seek God, to pursue him, comes not from us, but rather from God. We must pray for the grace of great desire for the Lord. God will give us this desire to seek him when we ask him for it, and then he will fulfill this desire as we come to know him and grow in his deep love, transformed through our communion with him.

I beg you, end my worries,
for no one else is able to,
and may my eyes finally see you,
you, who are their true light.
For I want to use them for you alone.

The soul continues to beg the Beloved to put an end to its sufferings and worries. It hopes to contemplate him with its interior eyes since he is its light and it only wants to use them for him alone. It says:

"I beg you, end my worries."

It is anguish that causes its thirst to see God, which it calls "worries" here, and only its possession of the Beloved alone could put an end to it. It also asks him to end them by his presence... "For no one else is able to."

In order to better move the Beloved and persuade him to fulfill its petition, the soul says that, since no one other than he could satisfy its need, it must, consequently, be him who will end its worries. It is noted that God is very ready to comfort the soul and remedy its problems when the soul neither has, nor seeks to have, any other satisfaction and comfort than Himself. The soul that can find no other relief than that from God cannot remain long without a visit from the Beloved.

"And may my eyes finally see you."

That is, let me see you face-to-face, with the eyes of my soul.

"You, who are their true light."

God is the supernatural light that illuminates the eyes of the soul. Deprived of this light, it is plunged into darkness. In an expression of affection, it calls its Beloved the light of its eyes, in the same way as lovers give this name to the one they love.

It is as if it said: since you are the only light of my eyes, by your nature and love, let them be allowed to contemplate you, the one who, in every way, is their light.

"For I want to use them for you alone" (CS 10:1–5).

To be with the person we love and who loves us, to taste the joy of being together is the profound desire that dwells in each of us. And if it could happen during their meetings, the silence would be richer than words, then we could discover the other or allow ourselves to be discovered by the other simply in a reciprocal welcome, in a well-understood contemplation. Is it not necessary to contemplate for a long time in order to reach the invisible, at the heart of the being? The more that a presence is desired, the more intense the desire becomes within us to want to live it. One who thirsts for the presence of God could reach the point of being *"consumed with desire."*

We must allow ourselves to be possessed with the desire of the presence of God to the point of being able to truly say: "Lord...your name and your renown are the soul's desire. My soul yearns for you in the night, my spirit within me earnestly seeks you..." (Isa 26:8–9). It is a desire that takes precedence over any other desire, no matter how noble it may be. It is the desire of a presence in which all others will be transformed and purified. But does this desire truly dwell within us? Do we have this aspiration in our life to contemplate God with our interior eyes? In fact, this desire does not come from ourselves or our own aspirations. It is fundamentally a gift from God. Perhaps we must first ask for it like we do for a choice grace. A certain prayer, repeated as much as is necessary, is sure to be fulfilled by God. Let us listen to what the Lord says: "Then when you call upon me and come and pray to me, I will hear you. When you search for me, you will find me; if you seek me with all your heart, I will let you find me..." (Jer 29:12–14).

To ardently petition and seek the God who allows you to find him is what frees one from anguishes and worries, that is to say, we must learn to see everything in God and with God and not only with our human eyes that have a vision that is too exterior. When God is present and we attribute everything to his presence, daily life, as it remains the same, is progressively transformed. God lets himself be found within us and even around us, if we allow ourselves to be entered and infused with the richness of his being, Love. It could not then be a furtive desire of an exterior presence. Consumed with desire, emptied of one's self in order to leave all the space there for God. Am I dreaming, aspiring to the surreal? No, since this desire to contemplate your presence, Lord, to taste your presence, is a gift of your love. And if I am worried about my inconstancy and lack of ardor, at times, you make me understand, Lord, that you will never leave me, and that you will never go far away from the one who never goes far from you. Then, give me this profound thirst to contemplate you, this aspiration to live off your presence. Only you, Lord, can satisfy the desire that I have for you.

It is true, on certain days I feel that I am overflowing with energy and courage to the point that I could believe that I am capable of something through my own means. However, my eyes will not open to the luminous light of your presence, my glance lacks depth; they will roam in the meandering shadows of the course of life. It is said: *"Know that your flesh is weak and that nothing that is in this world knows how to give your spirit vigor or consolation"* (ED, p. 203). Only you, Lord, are able to satisfy the desire I have for you.

The presence of God is the center of life, a source of peace and the hearth of light, it is a presence that bathes everything. Whoever calls upon this presence in the depth of his heart, puts all of his strength to love in God, and refuses to stop himself at passing, exterior satisfactions, is close to seeing his desire fulfilled. He is already partially consumed by all that is not God within him. He has already released what is useless to him in order to reach what is essential, God contemplated within him, but for God's sake, not his own. God comes to visit the one whose heart completely welcomes his coming. For God is also full of the desire to visit his creatures, the Beloved strongly aspires to fulfill, with his presence, the being who thirsts for his coming. In the depth of his tenderness, how could he make the soul who seeks the One it loves wait any longer? How can he not find joy in a heart that is free of all created things, thirsty for the presence of the Beloved, the Lord God? How could he not illuminate the soul, who finds no relief outside of him, for whom he is everything, the soul which has no other profound desire than the desire for God, with the gift of himself?

It is true that we have been made to see, for a face-to-face. It is thus that God created us, to be in a face-to-face, already in a closeness in our world, but also for the eternal face-to-face. Just like the only Son and Beloved, Jesus, we also have been made to turn our glances towards the Father, to be in a face-to-face with him, to taste and contemplate the infinite Beauty, the delicious Presence who fulfills and satisfies all purified desires. But already, now, *"may I see you, face-to-face, with the eyes of my soul"*?

May your light, you who are light, penetrate me, chase away the shadows of sin. May I, through your light, become conscious of the shadows that are within me and around me. Put, into my hands, the torch of the union with you, of communion with you so that I advance towards you, the light of faith that illuminates the intelligence, the light of hope that strengthens the will, the light of charity that conquers the heart. It is a light that melts away all reluctance and leads us to give of ourselves through the discovery of the presence of God, not of a faraway God, but a God with a face of tenderness who leads us to an intimate union with him. Tenderness brings tenderness. It is the Beloved who is present in the heart of the seeker of God. God is not afraid of man, for he became a man. My Beloved. Let us have no fear of these words which are an expression of the intensity of a human kind of love. Let us purify ourselves in God. How can we not give ourselves to God whom we cherish to the extent of being delivered by love, by loving the Beloved more than anything else? But we must always climb a mountain to get to that point, break away from everything that is not him in order to discover "his face (which) shone like the sun, and his clothes (which were) dazzling white" (Mt 17:2). My Beloved, unique light of my eyes, let me be consumed with the desire for your presence. I want to use my eyes for you alone with a glance of love that is illuminated by your own glance of love.

REFLECTION QUESTIONS

Everything comes from God. *Everything*. Even our earliest inclinations that we desire our Creator. God's grace is abundant, and it fuels us, moving us to seek the Lord in every corner of our lives. In what ways do I seek the Lord? In prayer? In action? Do I seek the Lord in my brothers and sisters in Christ? Is my desire for God so great that I seek the Lord in all things, in all people (despite differences of opinion), in all situations (regardless of how absent God may seem at that time)?

DAY FOUR

Wounded, Am I Totally Yours?

FOCUS POINT

We cannot divide our hearts between two treasures. We commit to one or the other; that which is God, or that which is not. If we give our hearts to God, we must give them without reserve. As we abandon our selfishness, we find the ultimate object of affection—God. Our hearts are enflamed with love, hurting, restlessly seeking the ultimate object of affection.

Why, since it is you who has wounded my heart,
have you refused to heal it?
And since you have robbed me of it,
why then have you left me like this
and not taken the stolen good?

The one who loves said that the object of his love has ravished his heart, and by that very fact, this heart is no longer his, but belongs to the person he loves.

The soul then knows if it loves God purely or not. By loving him in this way, the heart is no longer its own, it no longer thinks of its own pleasure or interests, but only of the glory, honor, and good pleasure of God. The more the heart is dispossessed of itself, the more it is occupied by God.

Here are two signs from which we could strongly recognize if God has truly ravished our heart. Is he the object of our ardent desires? Do we experience nothing outside of him? Our heart can only experience peace and rest if it has an object of affection. However, when it is strongly enamored, it neither possesses itself nor anything else. And if, on the other hand, it doesn't clearly possess the object of its love, its torment is in proportion to what it lacks, and it will endure it and not be fully satisfied until it completely possesses it. At that point, this soul could be compared to an empty vessel waiting to be filled or to a hungry person who wants food, or a sick person yearning for good health, or a person who is suspended in the air with no foothold. That is the condition of a heart that is enflamed with love.

This soul that has this experience says:

"Why, then, have you left me like this?"

That is so say: why have you left me empty, hungry, lonely, wounded, sick from love, and suspended in the air?

"And not taken the stolen good?"

Which is to say: why don't you take this heart, that love made you steal, with you so that you can fill it, satisfy it, in order to unite yourself to it, to return it to health, to give it perfect rest in you? (CS 9:4–6).

This is a good question to ask ourselves when we are seeking God and feel that we have been wounded by the love of God which has penetrated, consumed, and purified us through his presence. For, we must not let ourselves fall into that trap. The Lord hates shared hearts and lying lips. He wants our hearts for him alone, no matter what our vocation is in the Church. All human love must blossom in the love of God. It must even be human, incarnate, in order to be true and become divine. It will then pass beyond creation, in various stages: betrothed love, fraternal love, the love of being consecrated which calls for mediation. It is the mediation that differs, but it must never be the screen to give our heart to God. Otherwise, it would disfigure love. Our heart could finally be given totally only to God, because only he alone could fulfill a love, a created heart. "For where your treasure is, there your heart will be also" (Mt 6:21). Is God really my treasure? Has he fully ravished my heart and become everything in my life? We can already assess this and discover if God is everything in our lives if we give precedence, lighting the way, if everything we are and do converges towards him and if he is of primary importance—him, not us. The God of Love is the center of our love, its focal point, the outcome of our love. Him, nothing but him; me, everything for him, everything in him. Our first preoccupation is to love this God who is Love; our thoughts are totally taken over by the presence of the Beloved; our words are overflowing with the wealth of love given and received from above; our worry is to always please the Beloved and make him know that he is the only one capable of fulfilling a created heart. It is a disinterested love which is disencumbered of myself and all-welcoming to the Beloved, the God of Love. It is a pure, transparent love that doesn't seek satisfaction, joy, or personal interest for its own sake; it would even be the opposite of true love which would make us enclose ourselves and would destroy us by closing us up within ourselves. It is a love that is as pure as crystalline waters because it only seeks the good pleasure of God. It is a love that figures out what would make God happy. It is a love that gives God his proper glory, that honors him through the recognition of his own love which dwells within us and in which we love him in return. It is a love that is received from the Beloved in order to offer itself to him. For "...(his) power at work within us is able to accomplish abundantly far more than all we can ask or imagine" (Eph 3:20). Everything has its source in the Beloved and nothing could happen unless we have agreed to act in consequence. *"The more the heart is dispossessed of itself, the more it is occupied by God."* More...then, there are no limits on our human roads. To be freed from our self will always be a part of our aspiration to love more. God will occupy all that is dispossessed. And he will call us to descend into our interior being in order to disencumber ourselves, in a way so that he can occupy all of the space there: "...hurry and come down, for I must stay at your house today" (Lk 19:5). What a marvel! God, the Beloved, he who penetrates into my entire being if I offer him the entirety of my heart.

In order for us to avoid all illusion, for fear that we would remain there only through the feelings that vanish as quickly as they appear, two signs are offered to us so we can discover if God has truly ravished our heart.

"Is he the object of our ardent desires?" Each of us has noble desires which give us life: health, work, family, the community of life, the realization of projects; these are good as long as they are starting points to help us reach God. Here is the test to verify it: are they truly starting points or is one or another of them monopolizing? Ardor gives birth to desire,

and undertakes everything to satisfy it. Then, do our ardent desires make everything converge towards the sole ardent desire that overrides all other desires: to have our heart ravished by God, a heart that is totally reserved for him, a heart that finds all of its happiness in him, a heart that gives him happiness? "We know that all things work together for good for those who love God, who are called according to his purpose...he also predestined (them) to be conformed to the image of his Son..." (Rom 8:28–29). Therefore, a heart that is completely enflamed with the love of the Son for his Father. It is a fire that is lit by him in our heart. It is a love that is re ceived in order to be sent back to its source. Ardent desires to be verified in us that converge towards the only true desire, God.

"Do we experience nothing outside of him?" Let us not forget our human nature. All human beings, all hearts, have the need for an object of affection, without which it knows no peace or rest. But then it could love foolishly and lose control of everything. *"It neither possesses itself or anything else."* It is like a disoriented compass that is good for nothing because it can't point to the north. It is a heart that is enamored with everything that could disorient it along the path to God, with anything that could steer it away from its healthy vocation, a heart that cannot detach itself from created things, a heart that can no longer be available to love, a heart that is a prison of certain ideas or an ideology, a heart that is enamored that can neither experience God nor love him.

The heart is made to love the One it has discovered to be its everything in life and love, but which perceives what is lacking and empty in itself. *"It doesn't clearly possess the object of its love."* The torment will last as long as its dissatisfaction. And satisfaction will only come through complete possession.

But what emptiness? If it is emptied of God, that is as a result of it being filled with too many things, too many created encumbrances. God can only come into a soul that is emptied of all things, emptied of all strange love, disencumbered of itself. Perhaps we must take inventory of the encumbrances that we perceive within our hearts and our lives. And if God grants us the grace to see ourselves clearly, let us call upon him to help us realize this emptiness, for we need courage in order to do it. Let us also be aware that: "the one who began a good work among you will bring it to completion by the day of Jesus Christ" (Phil 1:6).

Emptied of ourselves in order to be filled with God. A vessel that is not destined to be empty. Its purpose is to be filled to the maximum with what can be put there. The empty stomach awaits food which will satisfy it. The sick person sighs as he seeks good health. The person with no support seeks a foothold. Completely emptied, all deficiencies call to what will bring them a remedy. Emptied of everything in order to be filled, fulfilled by the God of love. A heart enflamed with love that can no longer know the emptiness of creation so that it is fulfilled with God's bounty. A heart that is offered and given to love like a sacrificial altar wherein the offering of the Beloved passes the offering of the Beloved, from the soul consumed and penetrated by the burning love of his Lord.

But there are days when the wound is made vivid in our heart, this heart which God wants for himself alone. Why do the silences of the Beloved leave me famished for his love, emptied of his presence, sick from love, without rest before him? Would this not be an invitation from you, Lord, so that I can say to myself: In fact, am I totally yours, Lord; nothing but yours?

REFLECTION QUESTIONS

Where do I find the treasure in my life? Is my treasure my relationship with God? Do I seek this treasure by constant prayer, discerning God's will, and uniting my will to my Lord's? Are there obstacles in my life that prevent me from laying claim to this treasure? Are there impediments to my will uniting to God's will? How can I address these impediments? What action can I take in this regard?

Christ, to Discover Who You Are in Order to Be Yours

FOCUS POINT

Christ is the "abundant mine that contains innumerable treasures." As our Lord reveals himself to us in our lives, we discover more of our humanity and our capacity for divinity. He who is fully human and fully divine reveals all of this to us, and by discovering the humanity and divinity of Jesus Christ in ourselves we are drawn ever closer to its source, the Holy Trinity, and we are transformed within.

Then we climb from the rock
to the elevated caves.
These caves are well hidden,
and there, we enter,
we both will taste the sap of the pomegranate.

The stone, then, that is needed is Christ himself, according to what Saint Paul said: "...the rock was Christ" (1 Cor 10:4). The "elevated caves" of this rock are none other than the sublime and profound mysteries of the wisdom of God, hidden in Christ.... They are so elevated and so profound that they are rightly designated by the name "elevated caves": "elevated" because of the sublimity of the mysteries they contain, "caves" because of the profoundness of God's wisdom which we find contained there...

"These caves are well hidden."

They are so well hidden that the holy doctors who discover some of them and the privileged souls that have tasted amazing things in this life, can only explain a small part. Christ is like a huge cavern to be explored! He is an abundant mine that contains innumerable treasures; we can dig forever and yet never find the bottom. The more we extract from that mine, the more discoveries we will make of new veins which reveal other wealth.

That is what Saint Paul said when he spoke about Christ: "In whom are hidden all the treasures of wisdom and knowledge" (Col 2:3). In order to reach that point, the soul, of necessity, must first pass by the narrow path of interior and exterior suffering. That is the path that leads to wisdom. Yes, no one in this life can penetrate into the mysteries of Christ without suffering a great deal....

The soul truly wants to reach Christ's caves so that it may plunge itself into them, transform itself, and intoxicate itself with the love that they contain. But if it aspires to hide itself in the arms of the Beloved, he must invite it there (CS 37:1–5).

No one can reach your Mystery without difficulty, Lord, unless you invite them there and reveal yourself. We must agree to go and discover it and then know the difficulties to reach it and the happiness at our progress. We could think that the apostles were in a better place than we are, just as the disciples of the Lord. But what did they understand about you, Jesus, during your time here on earth? They did not penetrate into your mystery. They needed the faith of Easter and the penetrating light of the Holy Spirit so that their eyes would finally be opened. It is the same paschal faith that dwells within us, the Spirit of God gives its vibrant light and convincing warmth to our faith.

It will happen only if we make ourselves supplicants first: "I pray that the God of our Lord Jesus Christ, the Father of glory, may give you a spirit of wisdom and revelation as you come to know him, so that, with the eyes of your heart, enlightened, you may know what is the hope to which he has called you, what are the riches of his glorious inheritance among the saints" (Eph 1:17–18). All enlightenment comes from above. By welcoming it, we will be able to discover the entrance to the cave, penetrate it, travel through it, always going further and penetrating its depths, without leading us astray. In fact, it is the symbolism of the cave that we are offered in order to discover Christ and his mystery. Christ is the cornerstone and the foundation and building stone.

They are very well hidden caves, and we must discover the entrance. We cannot penetrate into Christ's mystery directly, without having taken the care to disengage ourselves from all of the obstacles that prevent us from finding it. We do not reach Christ's mystery without having allowed our hearts to have been prepared by the grace of the Lord. We can't come to God without first hearing his call, without making ourselves listen for it: "Everyone who has heard and learned from the Father comes to me" (Jn 6:45). Those are Jesus' words. I think that I understand all that I must do to prepare to discover you, Lord. Help me see what I must do. Then, infuse me with the courage to do it.

Here I am entering the cave. At first glance I ascertain that I must get used to looking at things in another way than from the outside and hold the lamp of the Holy Spirit, directing the luminous column in all directions. It is a cave that appears in all of its height and depth. The ways of access to reach the summit or the depths give me a sort of vertigo. What splendor! I must stop at the threshold in order to contemplate the breadth of what I see. I see mysteries that are so elevated and, at the same time, so very deep, that they are beyond my reach. And yet you invite me to enter so I can discover. My cry of amazement and contemplation could only be your own. I also borrow this phrase from you: "I thank you, Father, Lord of heaven and earth, because you have hidden these things from the wise and the intelligent and have revealed them to your infants; yes, Father, for such was your gracious will" (Lk 10:21).

Jesus, the reality of your Incarnation shows us your height and depth, as well as your humanity. The beauty of your human face, pleasant and peaceful, your penetrating glance which neither scrutinizes nor stares, but calls to the meeting by revealing its depth of love. Your hands that have so often been placed on the little ones and the sick, hands that have let the power of your grace escape, the power that heals, comforts, and encourages. Your words, some of which echo in my ears, call for me to always be a better disciple by following in your footsteps. Your feet that walked on our earth, this earth that is your creation, to unite with the poor, the marginalized, also carried you to spread your message of love. Your behavior is righteous and transparent, but also firm before those who opposed you and want to undermine your work and finally enclose themselves within their sins. The height and depth of your humanity was destroyed by an unjust condemnation, in which you carried all of our injustices upon your back; on your bruised and bloody face and your head, crowned with thorns. It is a Holy Face of love, disfigured. A wounded heart. Your body was subjected to atrocious suffering until your heart burst forth with its supreme cry: "It is finished" (Jn 19:30).

The height and depth of this humanity was glorified when the Father, by receiving your love as his Son on the cross, manifested his Fatherly love to you through your resurrection from the paschal sunrise. It was a humanity that was glorified from the heights of heaven. Sitting at the right side of the Father, you will reign forever. You are the Pontiff that will bind the earth to heaven. For all time, you are the unique Mediator and intercessor at the Father's side. O Holy Humanity of Christ, in your risen self, you fascinate me. As you set the Table with the new Easter, as you are present at the table of our Eucharists, you make me see the Table of the eternal Covenant at the celebration of your Marriage, in the new Kingdom. You fascinate me.

In this global discovery that amazes me, right from my entry, you invite me to penetrate into it entirely, step by step. More and more, I feel my powerlessness and my inability to descend all the way to the very depths and to climb to the summit. The wisdom that feeds this secret contemplation like a fertile source is "a language from a pure spirit to a pure spirit" (NO, p. 138), a language from God to man, your language of God to my soul. But how can I adapt to you, Lord, if you don't come to me yourself to help me adapt to you by purifying all of my being in a glance, by disengaging my heart of all its inability to love, and by giving me the capacity to go all the way to the Invisible by the gift of faith? You also teach me that I will never discover everything about you. You are so great, the cave so exceeds what my glance could discover about you. It is true, you are a cavern to explore. What amazes me even more is that no one can ever discover everything about you, but you give each of us the ability to perceive a small fragment of your mystery, on the condition that they welcome your Wisdom: the litany of the saints which are our predecessors in their witness. And when, by living together, we allow each thing that you have made us discover about you show through, we live of you, we vibrate in ourselves, giving thanks to have been next to those who have given us a spark of your mystery, thankful that you have given us the gift of having been given, along with the others, the spark of your mystery. Without a doubt, I must learn to discover this spark everywhere. I also know that I will never finish discovering, since the more I will love, the better I will love, and the more access you will give me to your other riches.

But one can't make profound discoveries or have access to your mystery without suffering, because there is no love without suffering. I will always work to agree with you and let myself be in agreement with you. That will necessitate my passage by the "narrow path of suffering," the rejection of everything that is not you, the abandonment of all false wisdoms, in order to reach the One Wisdom, you. I am called again to "interior and exterior suffering." I will unite myself, spirit, body, and soul. In each area I must cut back so I can be fully open.

If I, by grace, aspire to discover what you are, O Christ, it is in order to become yours. I proceed with confidence, in spite of my smallness, for I know that "you show yourself first to those who seek you. I know that you benignly come to meet them" (ED, p. 198). Plunge yourself into me. Hide me within you. Transform me in you.

REFLECTION QUESTIONS

In what ways does Jesus Christ reveal his humanity to me? What aspects of his humanity are most moving to me? His ability to listen? To relate to whomever he interacted with? To be wholly present to his audience? To speak the truth? In what ways does Jesus reveal to me the divinity inside myself? By showing that I am capable of forgiveness and deep love? In what ways am I transformed by Jesus Christ's revelation of his humanity and divinity?

How Can I Become Like You?

FOCUS POINT

Our human free will is key in becoming like God. Everything comes from God—the desire to love, the ability to love—but finally it comes to a personal decision to unite our will with God's will. We must strip our will of all selfishness, and surrender it freely to God. Nothing that opposes the divine will must remain in our own will.

When we speak about the union of the soul with God, we are not speaking of this substantial and primordial union between God and his creatures—God dwells substantially in all souls, even if they are the greatest sinners in the world—but of the union that is a transformation of the soul in God, a union that does not always exist, but only when there is a resemblance of love.

This happens when the two wills—that of the soul and

that of God—are so conformed together that there is nothing in the one that is repugnant to the other. Thus, once the soul totally rids itself of that which does not conform to the divine will, it is transformed in God through love.

God communicates himself most to the soul that is the richest in love; namely, the one that has its will in closest conformity to the will of God.

Therefore, the more completely a soul is wrapped up in creatures and its own abilities, the less preparation it has for such a union, for it doesn't give God the complete freedom to transform it supernaturally.

So that both these things may be better understood, let us make a comparison. A ray of sunlight strikes a window. If the window is misty or stained in any way, the rays of the sun will be unable to illuminate it and transform it into its own light totally, as it would if it were totally transparent and free from all stains, even more if it was pure. The problem is not with the ray of sunlight, but with the window.

But if it was totally clean and pure, the ray of sunshine will transform it and illuminate it in such ways that it will seem to be a ray itself and give off the same light as the ray. It is true that the window, even though it very much resembles the ray, has its own distinctive nature. However, we may say that the window has become a ray of light by participation (MC II, 5:3, 4, 6).

I f I aspire to become yours, Lord Jesus, because you have placed this profound desire within me, I must take the appropriate steps to reach you. I know, furthermore, that you support everything in man. What we are, we take from you. In you, we exist and are set into motion. Without you, it would be nothingness. You hold us in your hands and you are present to all human beings, as much for the greatest saint as for the greatest sinner. But what it takes is that we must become like you. And that is what you invite us to do: "walk before me and be blameless…and (you) will come to establish a covenant between you and me" (see Gen 17:1–21). First, I must agree to walk, yet never to settle down. I must walk in your presence, by receiving the strength from you to remain standing, the vision of the beginning of the itinerary to follow, and your words of encouragement. You will even go to the extent of forging a covenant with me, that is to say, to the extent of elevating me to a new relationship with you, so that I can become your partner in the covenant. My heart gushes with thanksgiving. The more profound it is in my being, the more I adhere to your covenant, the clearer the road you trace for me appears: the road of resemblance of love. God is love in his own mystery. It is love in the Father/Son relationship and Son/Father relationship. It is love in mutual giving, God's Holy Spirit. It is a resemblance of love, resemblance of a profound relationship, of giving and communion. It is not by fusion, but by participation with God, in a silence "at the deepest part of the substance of the soul" (VF, p. 227) where God confides in the soul that has become a total welcome to him, so much that it allows itself to be elevated all the way to God. Did he not make man in "the image of his own eternity" (Wis 2:23)? We are made to love through God who is love.

What remains is the question of "how?"—of what road to take so that we don't have any illusions, to know how to bring about the conformity of the two wills, God's and our own. More precisely, the conformity of our will with that of God. It is a road of the stripping of one's being, from the beginning, just like Christ did, by coming to this world: "See, God, I have come to do your will" (Heb 10:7). And we know just where that led him, all the way to the cross. It was a cross that sorely injured his Body just as it hurt his interior being. It was a cross that became the "yes" of love in communion with the will of the Father, and while waiting for when he would raise the dead, the Father manifested his own will of love and the recognition of that of the Son. It is a road of stripping oneself bare, the abandonment of ourselves for a conscious surrender, free and voluntary, into the hands of God. It is a stripping of everything that is not worthy of God in us and our lives. "What is born of the flesh is flesh, and what is born of the Spirit is spirit" (Jn 3:6). It will always be up to us to free ourselves and allow ourselves to be saved from what is only human within us, from all that would not have been grasped, crossed, and purified by the Spirit of God. It is a road of the stripping of everything that makes us "share Christ's sufferings" (see Phil 3:10) with the view of the newness of life in love with him. It is a harsh stripping of what we are, of what we want, in order to be plunged into the love of God and to find ourselves transformed by him. For to be clothed only by creatures and deliberately attached to everything that has been created in our lives cannot lead us to the depths of love. To be attached to our own abilities as if we were the sole master, does not bring us to the depths of love. It is a harsh stripping that takes precedence over all these attractions within us, all of the desires that dwell in us. All must be purified in order to become transparent with God.

For, if there must be a stripping of self, it is done to "clothe Christ" (see Col 3:10) and to be plunged into his own love. We feel the need to ask the Lord to help us so that "you may be filled with the knowledge of God's will in all spiritual wisdom and understanding" (Col 1:9). May he set us up in companionship with him so that we will become rich, ever richer with his filial love, with a communal love that puts us into a face-to-face of love with the Father. Did he not tell us that *"God communicates himself most to the soul that is the richest in love; namely, the one that has its will in closest conformity to the will of God"*? Rich with a love that comes from God and not from us. But also rich with a love that we have let penetrate ourselves as much as our heart is disposed to welcome it. It is a will that renders itself conformed to his because he allowed us to grasp what he wants from us and helps us live his own project of love within ourselves. The more we give God *"the freedom to make the necessary transformations, the supernatural transformations,"* the more we will give witness to our wealth of love and even more, we will have understood how to resemble Lord Jesus, by using his own road of offering which could be none other than the road of love. Perhaps we must allow ourselves to be more intensely inhabited by God, to become his preferred dwelling. That will happen for the one who loves and keeps the Word in his heart: "My Father will love them, and we will come to them and make our home with them" (Jn 14:23). We could say that only one concordance exists between the will of God and our own. We could say that we would have found the "how" to become like God by invigorating his children with his own life.

But nothing is ever acquired once and for all. We can't set ourselves up in love, we live it. It grows, it spreads, it always progresses, unless we let it dwindle. Perhaps we must distrust a restricted type of love, a heart that gives without surrendering itself, a will that is given only partially, a freedom that affirms itself, without fully building it. Loyally, before God, let us see if the window of our eyes, heart, will, freedom, and feelings would not be a little obscured, to the extent of not allowing the ray of the love of God to completely penetrate us. It is a window that is obscured by the clouds of lukewarmness, little by little, by a lack of generosity and nonchalance. It is a window that is obscured by the stains, small in themselves—we call them venial sins—but which result in impoverishing love, by preventing the sparks of love, by diminishing our ability to give of ourselves completely. In fact, to just about love something is not to love it at all. However, we are called to reach the union of wills to love . That "makes you strong with the strength of the Lord" (see Col 1:11). He is the powerful ray that offers himself to the window of our own love so that the God of love can diffuse his power to love within us, so that our life will be revealed as a reflection of love. God is God. We will remain his creatures. But, *"by our participation in love,"* through grace, we will come to resemble him. All of our being which has become transparent to God will receive him and send him back like a luminous sign, as if the window has disappeared; it will remain, however, as an attraction for love. *"It will send God back to God."*

REFLECTION QUESTIONS

What are the bad habits in my life that obstruct me from deeper communion with God? How can I wean myself from these habits? Might a more structured prayer life help me to focus more on my faith life, assisting me in avoiding the temptations of bad habits that hamper my spiritual life? Might I consider praying morning and evening prayer from the breviary as a start to a more structured prayer life?

DAY SEVEN

Going to You With All the Strength of My Will

FOCUS POINT

We must align our own will with that of God to such a degree that we cannot choose apart from what is good, from what is in accord with God's will. Our will must be strengthened with a commitment to meticulously stripping away all those things in our lives, eliminating those bad habits, which do not align themselves with God's will. Any string or cord which restricts our free will should be severed.

The state of the divine union consists of the soul's total transformation of its will into the will of God, so that there may be nothing in the soul that is contrary to the will of God, but that, in everything, what drives this human will is purely and absolutely the will of God.

...In this state of union of two wills, there is only one, to know the will of God is to become the will of God. If this soul desired any imperfection—something that God couldn't want— there would no longer be one will, since the soul wants something that God doesn't.

It is clear, then, that for the soul to unite itself perfectly with God through love and will, it must first be free of all voluntary desires of the will, no matter how slight. It must not intentionally and knowingly consent to any imperfections, and it must come to the point of no longer being able to consent to it unintentionally.

I mean knowingly, because unintentionally and unknowingly, or without having the power to do otherwise, it may fall into imperfections and venial sins. It is about these sins, not completely voluntary, that it is written: "For though they fall seven times, they will rise again" (Prov 24:16). For such sins as these, even in small things, any one suffices to impede union. I speak about a habit that one doesn't change....

No matter if a bird is held by a slender cord or by a heavy one, since, if it is slender, the bird will still be held as if it were a heavy one; as long as the cord doesn't break the bird couldn't fly away. It is true that the slender one is easier to break, still, easy as it may be, the bird will not fly away if it is not broken. And thus it is, if the soul has an attachment to anything, no matter how much virtue it possesses, it will not attain the freedom of the divine union (MC I, 11:2, 3, 4).

———

To want, to be able to want through the freedom of our existence, is what characterizes our human nature and gives our actions their full meaning. To be responsible for what

happens, and for what happens as a result of a free and abso-
lute will, so much so that it is possible here on earth. All of our
commitments are only meaningful when they are made with a
free will, by a being that is able to choose, to think about the
consequences of such a gift, and apt to, humbly and without
doubts, but courageously and deliberately, then take the path.

In terms of faith, there is no difference with respect to the
importance of the will in order to be responsible for it. But the
source differs. I am not alone to make the choice. I have let
God dwell within me: "it is no longer I who live, but it is Christ
who lives in me" (Gal 2:20). The God that created me free,
removes all the insufficiencies and limitations from my freedom and will, and gives my freedom full reign to function. He
doesn't negate my freedom. He doesn't want to make my decisions. He gives me the possibility to want what he wants. He
makes me capable of wanting what he wants and, by seizing
this ability through the complete freedom of my being, I want
what God wants. My will is transformed into his will. If this
happens, nothing is contrary to God in my free will. Everything is pure and righteous in that which pushes me to act like
God wants me to act. Is it not true that: *Only the operation
of the will is capable of union with God*" (MC III, p. 140)
since it means the complete gift of an existence? There is not a
fusion of two wills, but a profound union, a communion. That
is what we see on the horizon of a first purification: to lose
oneself in the will of God, to unite oneself with Divine Love,
to leave one's self to be united, in close communion with the
Other who is the Lord. To accept to be with God in order to
be, definitively, more ourselves, fully ourselves. But more than
this, all voluntary imperfections must disappear from our hori-
zons. We can't build ourselves, in fact, by wanting two contrary
things. God, who is all perfection, could not want imperfec-

tion. A human will that is closely united with his, then, could not want imperfection. Let us give this word "want" its full meaning, with all of the intensity that makes us responsible for ourselves and freely committed to the path of love. Let us also learn to recognize where and when there is *imperfection* for ourselves. Let us discover the incompleteness of our spiritual building, but also its deficiencies, perhaps its failings, its lack of finishing. It is a conformity with him that the Lord awaits from us. A conformity that is, initially, a grace. "I press on to make it my own, because Jesus Christ has made me his own" (Phil 3:12). Because Christ gave us the ability to understand, this understanding within us welcomes—which depends upon its discovery in order to do it—purification to operate in our life in order to want what God wants. However, God, who is Love, only wants it out of love. So that we can want to do it out of love, we must look at what we are, discover the obstacles that prevent our forward advancement, and *"be free of all voluntary desires of the will, no matter how slight."* These desires include all attachments, satisfactions, and affections that are stained with imperfection when they lean towards a sensory or spiritual good and when the will appropriates them deliberately and habitually. And the full union of will, ours with God's, necessitates not only that *"we must not intentionally and knowingly consent to any imperfections,"* but even more, it calls upon us so that *"it must come to the point of no longer being able to consent to it unintentionally."* What a purification of the depths of our being this exacts, it is true. But this must not scare us. To the contrary, this vibrant call of communion that God addresses to us reveals our grandeur to us and to just how far God wants to lead us. *"A single thought by Man is worth more than the entire world; it is for that reason that only God is worthy of it"* (ED, p. 202). That is what comforts in the operation of purification, in order to open us to a future, our future with God. Then, *"straining forward to what lies ahead, I press on toward the goal..."* (Phil 3:13–14). Halfheartedness has no place here, neither does the lack of will. It is always further ahead, further away, higher, with a will that controls the being, by governing all of the voluntary desires in order to reach the goal of a more profound union, but only after numerous purifications.

Perhaps someone could say: *"It is so high that I cannot attain it"* (Ps 139:6). Alone, that is true. But these words give us assurance: *"Abide in me as I abide in you.... Abide in my love. If you keep my commandments, you will abide in my love..."* (Jn 15:4, 9–10). To abide in love because it is offered to the love of the One who is Love. To abide in love, by being as attentive to the commandments as to the smallest signs and to the smallest desires. Remain attentive and vigilant, with the humility of the servant and firm confidence in Jesus who prayed at his ultimate hour about his personal offering so that we would be holy, created in the image of God. Not a superficial holiness, one of words, but a holiness in truth, through the union of our free will to the plentiful will of God: *"Sanctify them in the truth; your word is truth.... And for their sakes, I sanctify myself, so that they may also be sanctified in truth"* (Jn 17:17, 19). So everything that is an inadvertent weakness, uncontrolled imperfection, and venial sin must be plunged into the sanctifying actions of Christ who restores everything in us. The discovery of these weaknesses, even those of just men, must not discourage us, on the condition that we don't remain mired in it, but pick ourselves up, humble, but trusting in the God who abides in us and calls us to abide in his love. In the meantime, keep watchful, for certain *voluntary desires, no matter how slight*, of these inclinations or attachments to some sensory or spiritual good that may creep into us, when not controlled, that may constitute an obstacle to the full union with God. Self-control is just like a battle so that we can find our true freedom once again: a habit that we don't eliminate will quickly become a form of slavery. And without free will, we cannot please God, we cannot commune with God. *"The one who refuses to allow the elimination and stripping of his own will from himself...he will never find the Beloved"* (NO, p. 164). He allows himself to be sought and found by a heart that made the unique choice to give himself with a free and responsible will.

It is possible that a string holds me back by preventing me from being completely with God with all of the strength of my will. Even if it was a cord, we must not be discouraged. Both a string and a cord can be cut, although it is more difficult to cut a cord. In any event, we must sever the attachment that removes our true free will. Without that, the union with God would be impossible. Purification is necessary and must always be sought in order to experience the joy of living in love, with God who is Love, and to abide in his love. To purify oneself in order to love better, that is already to love and to be sure to be loved by the God of Love.

REFLECTION QUESTIONS

What actions, what methods do I take in my life to strip away the selfishness in me that separates my will from God's? Do I make a conscious commitment to weed out this selfishness on a daily basis? Am I sometimes too scrupulous, too hard on myself, as regards my attention to sin and selfishness in my life? How might I address these issues if they are present in my life? Might I consult my parish priest or spiritual director?

DAY EIGHT

My Path Could Only Be Yours

FOCUS POINT

We are called to follow the path of Christ. This is the path of love. This path will know feelings of joy and distress, union and abandonment, for all of this was a part of Jesus Christ's path. The God-made-man revealed to us what it means to truly live, and we should seek no other path than the one he has laid out before us.

"For the gate is narrow and the road is hard that leads to life, and there are few who find it" (Mt 7:14).

Oh, if one could only tell how much Our Lord desires this self-denial to be carried out! Yes, in truth, it must go all the way to a kind of death and annihilation of all things, temporal, natural, and spiritual: with respect to how much the will esteems it. Everything is there.

And this is what Our Lord meant when he said: "For those

who want to save their life will lose it." The one, he says, who
wants to seek or possess anything for himself, will lose it: "and
those that lose their life for my sake, and for the sake of the
gospel, will save it" (Mk 8:35)....

I couldn't call those who seek the soft and easy way and
refuse to imitate Christ good people....

We see that, at the moment of his death, Christ was aban-
doned and annihilated in his soul. His Father deprived him of
all relief and consolation, since he left him in the most inti-
mate aridity, which forced him to cry out, on the cross: "My
God, my God, why have you forsaken me?" (Mt 27:46). This
was the greatest spiritual desolation that he suffered in his life.
And it was also at this moment that he accomplished the great-
est work that he had ever done, a work that was superior
to all the miracles and marvels, either on earth or in heaven,
that he had done in his life: to know the reconciliation and
union of mankind, through grace, with God. And this work
was accomplished the moment and the time when this Lord
was most completely annihilated in everything. Annihilated,
that is to say, with respect to his human reputation, since, when
men saw him die on the cross, they mocked him rather than
esteeming him;...and further, with respect to the spiritual con-
solation and protection that he could hope for from his Father,
since He had forsaken him, so that he might pay man's debt
and unite him with God, being annihilated and reduced to
nothing himself (MC II, 7:6, 11).

F ollowing in the wake of Jesus, there could not be a question of volunteerism. It is an obedience that is assumed and
offered which opens Christ's path to us as our own. That ren-

ders us very humble, for everything comes from God at the same time as everything is attributed to us. God does not assume our role; he only calls us to humbly stay in our place and keep to it. He does not expect virtuous performances from us. Rather, he hopes to see us partake of the path that he trod first on man's territory. He *"doesn't look upon the greatness of our soul, but the greatness of his humility"* (ED, p. 209). This greatness of humility is a paradox. And yet, when we come to this purification of ourselves, all the way to being void of ourselves, then God can accomplish his work within us. For the true purification of our will goes all the way to *"a kind of death and annihilation of all things, temporal, natural, and spiritual, with respect to how much the will esteems it."* All of the areas of our life are touched at the same time, since our being is only singular. We go completely to God, as Christ did. *"A kind of death and annihilation with respect to how much it esteems it,"* with respect to the scale of values, with respect to what we do with it. We will find the supreme value in the very behavior of Christ. Everything else does not have to be depreciated, nor does it have to be overestimated. We have to esteem Christ, his righteous value, whether it is in our work realities, from what we assume in service to the groups we belong to, whether it is about our own abilities which are either innate or acquired, or, finally, whether it is the degree that we have reached on the scale of holiness. *Everything is there.* In the recognition of what we are, what we owe to God, in our attitude of humility before God, in the true depth of this humility, thanks to which God will be able to build us and make us become a completed being. Without a doubt, certain purifications are still necessary.

If we are truly in agreement that our path could be no other than the one taken by Jesus Christ, let us go over the conditions given for access to it: to lose in order to save. To lose oneself, then *"to not seek or possess anything for himself"*; and to not *"seek the soft and easy way"* of life. But to accept everything through humility, as if by possessing nothing, detached from everything, yet respectful of our environment, dead to all that is not God, in order to live of him, in order to blossom in him. Since Christ's path becomes our own path, we must be "imitators of God...and live in love (follow the path of love)" (Eph 5:1, 2). What is this path of love? It is the royal path of the cross, the cross that Christ was the first to welcome onto his shoulders, by inviting us to: "take up their (our) daily cross and follow..." (Lk 9:23). "He...endured the cross, disregarding its shame...(and) endured such hostility against himself from sinners..." (Heb 12:2, 3); he who "gave himself up for us" (Eph 5:2) because he loved us. If the Son's cross is truly a response of filial love, and, at the same time, a call of love from the Father, if the cross could be called the meeting of two loves, the love of the Father and of the Son, this love would however have been harshly suffered. On the cross, Jesus knew the most severe desolation: the Father's silence, *intimate aridity,* like a kind of absence. He even expressed it, by making Psalm 22 truly become the cry of a man in a profound situation of distress: *My God, why have you forsaken me?* On our path, in the wake of Jesus, we will also know moments of abandonment, distress, and spiritual darkness ourselves.

Will we always be able to shout a cry to God from the deepest parts of ourselves? For to cry out to someone is to cry out to God, it is to again recognize that he is there, even when he lets himself be sought. And if we then look at the cross, the crucified one? It is then that we must "look to Jesus, the pioneer and perfecter of our faith...and run with perseverance the race that is set before us" (Heb 12:1, 2). Christ resolutely went all of the way to the end and we, through grace, follow the path in order to withstand the trial.

The cross was Christ's *greatest work*. It was by the cross that he reconciled man with his God. For man, the cross has become the source of grace and the path of union with God. We must learn and relearn to look at the cross, taking it into our hands in order to discover that, planted into the ground, but lifted to the heavens, it re-established communication between man and God forevermore. God-made-man died on the cross, nailed to both the vertical and horizontal bars. At the junction of these two bars, was the heart of God-made-man. From its opening flowed living love. Grasped once again in our lives, it restores us in the love that comes from above. This could only be accomplished for us in the interior of ourselves, in a tearing away, an annihilation of ourselves, a sincere purification of our will as a way to answer "yes" in the true freedom of love.

The cross cannot be seen but through love, as a sign from God that saves and purifies man, like a sign from Jesus that changes his free will into the source and way of salvation for man. Without love, the cross has no significance. For the majority of witnesses, it was only an annihilation and failure, an object of scorn and low esteem. It was the death of a dissident, a blasphemer, an impostor. For God's chosen people, it in no way corresponded to the commitment they made, to their ideas about tomorrow. Suddenly, their hopes were dashed. What would become of the promise of faithfulness? For Mary, the Virgin Mother, was this not a harsh trial of faith? Only she alone, the one who was filled with grace, remained filled with love. The Son had truly stated: "unless a grain of wheat falls into the earth and dies, it remains just a single grain; but if it dies, it bears much fruit" (Jn 12:24). And on the cross, he lived this death that was the carrier of abundant fruit for all of humanity and for God, but he experienced this death in solitude: *"annihilated and reduced to nothing."* Reduced to nothing by the men who had nailed him to the cross. Annihilated by the silence of God. And yet, in and through that, came a marvelous source of grace flowing with eternal life for all men under heaven.

The cross lights our crosses. We must then deepen our opinion of the cross. *"May the crucified Christ suffice for you"* (ED, p. 208). We have the supreme proof of a salvational and redeeming love. There, we have the open book of God's love that the Scripture presents to us. There, we have the source of all purification in order to always be reintegrated in love. There, we have the sign of a will that was completely available to the Father, a call for us to invite God onto our path so that he will strengthen our wavering will and enlighten our choices. *"May the crucified Christ suffice for you, with him, labor and rest"* (ED, p. 208). There are times that are so difficult on the earthly path. There are moments of human and spiritual distress.

"Consider him who endured such hostility against himself from sinners, so that you may not grow weary or lose heart" (Heb 12:3). Grow weary through weariness. If this happens, let us come to seek our rest close to Jesus. *"It suited the Master to be like the disciple"* (MC II, p. 105). Just like God-made-man understood us, he will comfort us. But God will not make our decisions for us. Through him, our purified will will truly be free and thus truly able to make constructive choices and, at the same time, painful ones at times. Let us not delude ourselves. *"If you want to possess Christ, never seek him without the cross"* (ED, p. 296). But let us be reminded that the cross can only be seen in love, as a sign of love.

REFLECTION QUESTIONS
When I follow the path of Christ I feel joy and sadness, and a whole host of emotions in between. How do I respond in my faith life to these high and lows? Especially regarding the lows, the sad moments of my life, how do I encounter God at these times? Is there an increase or a decrease in my faith during these difficult periods? If my faith wavers during the lows of my life, might I make such times an opportunity to strengthen my relationship with God through prayerful listening?

DAY NINE

Purify My Knowledge

As humans, we are blessed with the capacity of knowledge. This knowledge helps us to determine what is good and what is bad for us in our lives as we seek the Lord. And our will acts on this knowledge. But without God's grace, God's purifying grace, our knowledge is not enough to ideally assist our will in seeking God. Our knowledge helps us understand God to some degree, but when our knowledge presupposes an understanding of God, or causes us to believe that we wholly understand God, we must call on God's grace to purify our knowledge and keep us humble in our lives.

The understanding will carefully avoid allowing itself to be interfered with or enticed by certain kinds of knowledge, imaginary visions, no matter what form they may take, when they present themselves with an image or a particular intelligence of sorts, whether they are false and come from the devil, or whether they are found to be manifestly true and coming from God. In no case should the soul admit to them and make them its own, so that it can remain detached, stripped, pure and simple, with no mode or manner of being, that is what is required for the union.

The reason for this is that all these forms make it perceptible to the means of the modes and manners of limitations. However, the Wisdom of God, to which the understanding must unite itself, has neither mode nor manner, it has no limitations or intelligence that are distinct and particular, and so that these two extremes—divine Wisdom and the soul—can come to be united, it is necessary that each conforms to the other in a certain way through a certain resemblance. It is necessary, then, for the soul to also be pure and simple, neither hampered by nor modified by any kind of limitation of form, species, or image. Since God is not subject to this limitation, the soul, in order to enter into contact with him, must no longer take on any distinct form or image.

What is known about this sublime state of union is that God does not communicate himself to the soul under the disguise of an imaginary vision, or representation of a figure. The way that God and the soul communicate is mouth-to-mouth, that is to say, the pure and naked essence of God—which is the mouth of God in love—with the pure and naked essence of the soul—which is the mouth of the soul in love of God.

...It (the soul) must then constantly turn its gaze away from all distinctive knowledge which comes to it through the sensory faculties and which don't take its means of support from the assured foundation of faith, in order to cast its gaze on what can't be seen or felt by the senses, but to the spirit, which can't be expressed by any sensory form, and in a phrase, to

*that which leads it to the union by the path of faith, which is
the true means for this union (MC II, 16:7, 9, 12).*

———

Lord, it is true that you gave man intelligence, this faculty of
the spirit which characterizes the human being, permitting
him to reason and make deductions and conclusions of all kinds.
In the midst of this creation, in its beautiful orderliness, just as
in the world of thought, I can discover you, Lord. But I only
have access to one part of your mystery. In order to penetrate
into the depths, I await everything from you. "No one can
come to me unless it is granted by the Father" (Jn 6:65). That
is the experience that I have already had in order to come to
this point. How I desire the Wisdom that only comes from
you, that which I will receive through the filial fear of you, the
one who "is wisdom and discipline" (Sir 1:27). On my path
there is no lack of beautiful creations of the spirit that I could
forge for myself, of well explained knowledge, as well con-
structed as I could build. But from where are they coming to
me? Are they coming from the spirit of lies disguised as an
angel of light? Are they coming from the Spirit of God himself? Discernment imposes itself upon me, but it is difficult. I
do know that *"intelligence, in order to be in a state of union
with the light (God) and to become divine, and in a state of
perfection, (needs to be) purified beforehand, annihilated with
respect to its natural lights"* (NO, p. 105).

It is as good as saying that I must "put away my former
self...to be renewed in the spirit of my mind and clothed with
the new self" (see Eph 4:22–24). In order to reach the state of
union with God, in intimate communion with him, in fact, it is
not the brilliant intellectual faculties that I will need, but "love

that overflows more and more with knowledge and full insight to help determine what is best..." (see Phil 1:9–10). My soul must remain *"detached, stripped, pure and simple."* It is the necessary purification in order to attain the union. Detached, without any means of access to God who chooses those he destines me to, by welcoming those that he makes available on my path as signs of his presence and love. Stripped, separated from my preconceived ideas, from my beautiful and knowledgeable constructions, in a way so that I am able to receive the light of God, the knowledge of the depths. Pure, without allegation, we could say, without human support, without that which comes from our ordinary abilities to think, since we are not of the order of discourse about God, but of the order of union which originates with God. Simple, without all the subtle deductions of knowledge and discussion, without the clever quibbles of argumentation. But then, Lord, why have you given me intelligence if I can't use it to communicate with you? You can't scorn what you have created yourself. You can't reject the beautiful intelligence of man when he is engaged in digging into your mystery. But you scorn and reject nothing. Very simply, you tell me that only my intellectual strengths are not the path of access to you, no matter how brilliant they are. You ask me to re-experience what the prophet Elijah did. You are not in the hurricane of our beautiful striking phrases; you are not in the earthquake of our shattering diatribes; you are not in the fire of our prophetic discussions. Lord, where are you then? "In the silence of a breeze" (see 1 Kings 19 passim), in this breath that is light and quivering which invades all beings and envelopes them and brings well-being and peace. A light breeze that is continuous, not just passing by. It is the presence of your Spirit, the gift of intelligence, light, and peace.

It is obvious that I can't imagine you would conform yourself to me, Lord. It is just the opposite: you come so that I can conform myself to you. My ways are not suitable to you. And so that I can conform myself to you, I must borrow your own ways. *"It is necessary that each conforms to the other in a certain way through a certain resemblance."* To be conformed to you through a certain resemblance to you, by being *pure and simple*, by allowing myself to be taught by you, disengaged from all of my theories, in an open simplicity, able to welcome what you want me to know about you. How can we not be aware, at the same time, that this is necessary for a meeting of the *two extremes*: you, Lord, the divine Wisdom, and I, a limited and finite being? It is not up to me to impose rules for the meeting, especially as you, in your tactfulness, propose them very simply. You surpass, from all of your immensity, all that I could imagine or build in my own representations. You call me, then, to reject all limitations, to not fabricate images or concepts, to not build idols which could be fraudulent about what you are. All representations that I could make of you, all imaginary visions, all forms, no matter how amazing, do not lead me to you.

We are all called to strip ourselves bare of our selves. It is the purification to which we are all called. *"Faith alone is the true means for the union with God,"* faith, which, in its first movement, has total confidence in God who reveals himself, says the faithful "yes" of a heart that loves, in the hope of perfection, all throughout its discovery of God. Faith which will call upon the support of an open intelligence, without ever forgetting that the knowledge of God does not merge with human knowledge. It is a paradox to affirm that *"the soul reaches God not by understanding, but by not understanding"* (VF, p. 200). And yet, it could not be otherwise than by our very human nature. The finite could not understand the infinite. By not being able to understand, I am thrown into faith, into the stripping of all my certainties that have intelligently been built in order to finally reach a discovery of God, by transcending what is close, of God, the All-Everything who calls me to a profound union with him. By not being able to understand, in the true meaning of the term, but to seize the intimate presence which abides in us through faith. It is an intimate knowledge through faith, then our intelligence becomes unhinged by the realities that go beyond it. The marvel of faith in a purified intelligence. "But those who do what is true come to the light..." (Jn 3:21). Lord, give me the courage to instill the truth within myself, to strip myself of a knowledge which presupposes to enclose you within my intellectual constructions. Open me to your truth, the one from which the light of faith flows forth for me, "yes" to what you are, in the most intimate part of my being.

A stripping of everything that comes to us through our sensory faculties. A stripping of everything that we could acquire through our senses. A disengagement from all that our spirit could erect about God. A disengagement from all that could come through sensory means. Not that they would be bad, since you made us this way with a human nature, since you call us to progress from the visible to the invisible, since you rendered yourself visible to our eyes in your real Human Body, but so that we will discover your own mystery as the Son of God. And the Scriptures repeat throughout that only the humble, poor, and the little ones can understand. Only those who abandon themselves to you through faith reach the Invisible. *"It is under the shadow of faith that intelligence unites itself with God"* (MC II, p. 129). It is to believe without seeing and yet, to carry within oneself a light that never goes out.

The purification of intelligence is accomplished definitively, through the gift of Love from God that the soul in love accepts. *"The way that God and the soul communicate is mouth-to-mouth,"* when God's gift, his breath of life, the purity of love, penetrates into the heart that is thirsty for God, freeing it from all sufficiencies, from all that will only be flesh, in order to make it a heart in love with God.

REFLECTION QUESTIONS

What methods do I employ to increase my knowledge and understanding of God? Might I choose to participate in weekly Scripture study? Make a daily habit of reading about the lives of the saints? Subscribe to a monthly religious publication? In what ways do my methods of better understanding God aid me in my prayer life?

DAY TEN

Christ, While I Am on the Path, You Are My Only Support

FOCUS POINT

The Word was spoken from the beginning, and it continues to resonate and sustain creation throughout eternity. "Give us, O Lord, our daily bread." On the path of life, the path we are called to travel, we are given sustenance by the Bread of Life, Jesus Christ. He is all we need on our travels, he sustains us without wanting. We need not call on anyone else.

It is not permissible for any creature to get out of the natural limitations that God has laid out for it in order to guide it. He gave limits to man that are natural and reasonable for the conduct of his life. It is then not permissible for him to seek to exceed them. However, to strive to know and recognize (them) by a supernatural path is to exceed the natural limitations.

That is, therefore, something not permissible, and consequently, it displeases God, for everything that is not permissible offends him....

Presently, faith is founded on Christ, we are in an era of grace....

By giving us his Son, as he has done, his Son that is the unique Word—for there is no other—God told us everything, all at this one time, through this Word, and he has nothing further to say.

As a consequence, God can answer the one who now wants to interrogate him: "If you want to hear a word of consolation from my lips, look at my Son who submitted himself to me and, through love, gave himself up to humiliation and affliction and you will see all the answers he will give you. If you want me to uncover some hidden things or a certain event, cast your eyes on him and you will find enclosed within him some very profound mysteries, a wisdom and God's marvels, by following this word of my Apostle: 'In him, he who is the Son of God, are hidden all of the treasures of wisdom and knowledge of God.' These treasures of wisdom will be more subtle for you, more savory and more useful than the totality of anything you could learn elsewhere." The same Apostle also boasted "to not know anything other than Jesus Christ and him crucified" (1 Cor 2:2)....

What we must do is let ourselves be guided by the law of Christ, God-made-man, and the law of his Church, which teaches us exteriorly and visibly through its ministers. It is by this very assured path that we will alleviate our ignorance and spiritual weaknesses. Through it, we will find the necessary help for all our needs (MC II, 21:1ff).

I know the limitations of my intelligence. And, from you, I learn, after having reflected and prayed to you that all of my knowledge about you comes from you. You do not provision me for a long period. "Morning by morning he wakens—wakens my ear to listen as those who are taught. The Lord God has opened my ear..." (Isa 50:4–5). These are the limitations you have established for me; a daily step-by-step with you. The great distances and journeys are not for me. Those will be limits that I won't know how to reach. Furthermore, if I go there, that would be displeasing to you since it would be to misunderstand the love that you give me moment after moment, in my small allocation. In creation, everyone respects the limits that you have assigned. What a risk I would run if I presuppose to go beyond what you want for me. *"That is something that is not permissible and everything that is not permissible offends you."* Make me understand well that I must limit myself to the path that you have invited me to pursue, very simply because you are there and not on the sidelines, because you are there and you give witness to me of your love and I can respond to you there, not from the sidelines. Open my ears so that I can hear, upon my awakening, your call to love, so that I can listen to what you reveal to me, in order to respond to what you expect of me.

Ours is a walk in faith, a faith that is enlightened by a Word, a faith that is nourished by a Word that we are called to welcome into our lives. And this Word of life "comes from the mouth of God" (Mt 4:4). It is the Incarnate Word. "In the beginning was the Word, and the Word was with God, and the Word was God" (Jn 1:1). *The Father spoke this Word who was his Son. He always spoke in an eternal silence.* No need to repeat it, for it reverberates throughout the ages like an echo. It spreads like the concentric circles of a wave; its vibrations continue to reach whoever is listening, whoever is able to grasp what is said. This necessitates that we will be beings of silence. It is in silence that the soul (our being) hears him, when all exterior and interior noises are deadened, when our will, intelligence, and memory, like all of the other senses, have been purified and appeased. It is the purification of my intelligence that silence has established, a silence that is not an absence of noise, but a bounty of peace.

For a being who is silence, one single word suffices when it is the word of the depths changing the other in his particular relationship with us. It is in this way that God, the Father, gave us his Son, his only Word, the founding Word of our life. We welcome this founding Word into ourselves in the resonance of faith, through a faith that takes its support from the Rock of this Word. It is a Word that is not exterior to us but abides within us: "it is in your mouth and in your heart..." (Deut 30:14).

These relationships of the depths are those of the Father with us through his Son. We live in an *"era of grace,"* a time of unending gifts from God which the Son brought us; a time of recognition about this God who places points of reference along our path of his Word in the Gospel. It is an era of grace which presents us with the open book of the cross. There *"God told us everything, all at this one time, through this Word, and he has nothing further to say."* It is a book that I can only read in the silence of love, the ardor of faith, and the solemnity of the heart. God has nothing further to say, but I have everything to learn from him. Everything is said in the open book of the cross; the reading in each instant is for us who live in the time, according to the limits that the Lord wants.

"This is my beloved Son who has all of my favor." These are the words of the Father about Jesus, prophetic and annuncia-

tor words. "You will do well to be attentive to this as to a lamp shining in a dark place, until the day dawns and the morning star rises in your hearts" (2 Pet 1:19). They are words that invite me to cast my gaze towards the Son on the cross, into his mystery of love where all enlightenment flows for my path. All that remains for me to do is question by looking and contemplating, for Jesus is the sole firm support for my faith.

Do I need words of consolation? The cross stands as a sign of the submission of the Son. Not the submission of a slave, but that of a Son. If not, what value does it have? Submission, in other words, obedience, and obedience that only makes sense when it is free and voluntary. The cross is a sign of humiliation and affliction. Humiliation about the situation as a slave with respect to life and death. Affliction born from physical and moral pain. At a time of pain, searching, and consolation, I am called here to seek the response of the cross. *"My Son who submitted himself to me through love."* That is the answer. From a situation that has no meaning to us, like all suffering, is born a new behavior and new meaning because love is there. Consolation is not obtained through asking for pity or by crying, even if we must submit to it, as the pain is so great. It is born out of the love which gives and re-gives meaning to what we are in the process of living. But only faith, which is a gift from God, can, in this case, lead us to a response of love, to an evaluation of events through love.

Do I need to discover the hidden meaning of things or seize the flow of the events that happen to me? The Father tells me: *"If you want me to uncover some hidden things or a certain event, cast your eyes on him (Jesus) and you will find enclosed within him some very profound mysteries."* From the manger to the crucifixion, on the roads of Palestine, listening to the little ones, the poor and the ill, just as in the battles against the powerful, it is so disturbing. We believed that man was in charge of all occurrences, when it is the Lord who is the Master of everything. Man gives the impression of triumphing when everything that he has done has failed. In fact, it is God who is the victor, but through the force of love. My intelligence doesn't penetrate all of his marvels at a first attempt. Moreover, how could it without the light from above, without the purification of all sensory resources and imagination? It is necessary for "the word of Christ (to) dwell in you richly..." (Col 3:16) so that we could have an intuition of the marvels of God. It is necessary for us to "learn wisdom" (Wis 6:9), for us to allow ourselves to be taught like the disciples in order to discover, in the life of Christ, through the means of the Gospel, the *"Wisdom and marvels of God."* They are treasures that are savory, sublime, and useful which the seeker of God discovers, whose intelligence is not satisfied to just discuss God, but who opens himself widely to the gifts of God, through a knowledge which leads to love. True knowledge is to know the crucified Christ, the Lord of Glory with our hearts!

"Trust in the Lord forever, for in the Lord God you have an everlasting rock" (Isa 26:4). He is the guide and true support. So that we have no illusions, Christ left us his law, the one of God-made-man, that his witnesses wrote into the Gospel. It is a law of love, justice, and peace. He entrusted his Church to *"teach us exteriorly and visibly through its ministers,"* those from whom we have the right to hear the Word of faith, love and forgiveness, as an explanation of the book of life in the light of God. *"The path united to the law of God and the Church to live through faith, obscure and true, in certain hope, and in perfect charity"* (ED, p. 293). We are, at times, opposed to this or we separate Christ from the Church. However, it is all one in the mystery.

Each person draws from the well according to what is in the mysteries of Christ. But there lies the true and sure support.

REFLECTION QUESTIONS

In my daily life, when temptations arise, what methods do I use to combat these obstacles? Do I call upon the Lord in prayer during these moments? Do I regard my daily prayer as the "daily bread" that sustains and nourishes me throughout my life? In what ways can I become more focused on this reality? What means can I take to strengthen my daily prayer life?

In Order to Get Close to You, I Must Rid Myself of Everything

FOCUS POINT

We can know God in silence. By stripping away noisy distractions, preconceived notions that shout out ignorant assumptions about reality, we can come to know God in the silence of our opened, uncluttered hearts. If we pray to be emptied of everything that is not God, only God will remain. God gives us the grace to empty ourselves of everything that is not God, so that we will desire and open ourselves only to God.

The memory must unite itself with God. From then on, it must necessarily void itself with respect to all forms (of knowledge) that are not God, since God doesn't fall under any distinct form or knowledge....

Then, the memory cannot be perfectly united with God if it is, at the same time, united with distinct forms and knowledge. In God, there are neither forms nor images which could be perceived by the memory. Also, when this strength is united to God, it finds itself stripped of all form and figure and its imaginary faculty is suspended. In a phrase, the memory is then plunged into supreme good, profound lapse of memory, remembering nothing....

The more that the memory is united with God, the more it loses sight of distinct knowledge, all the way to stripping itself of them entirely; that is what happens when it attains this perfect state of union....

One's elevation to this supernatural state could only be the work of God, but the soul could be prepared for it, that is within its power to do with God's help, and God puts it progressively into the possession of the union according to its own effort in this negation and privation of all form....

The spiritual being must habitually avoid collecting and storing in his memory all that he sees, hears, smells, tastes, touches, and let it quickly fall into a lapse of memory. May he put, if necessary, as much energy into forgetting them as others put into remembering them, in such a way that, in his memory, no knowledge or figure of what he has perceived remains as absolutely as if they had never existed. He must keep his memory completely free, without any reflections, neither about the things above nor about the things down below....

If the spiritual person does not believe, above everything else, that he will benefit from this suppression of knowledge and forms, he must not get discouraged. God will make him know what he will do in his own time. Furthermore, when it concerns such a precious blessing, it is righteous to suffer in patience, wait and hope (MC III, 2:4, 8, 13, 14, 15).

Here, I am called to purify my memory and even make a void in myself. Is it possible? Then, is it reasonable? What is my memory if it isn't this faculty that presents the past to me as if it is the present, if it isn't this faculty where one has the ability for his psychological states to come to his consciousness? But God is beyond all of this. *"God doesn't fall under any distinct form or knowledge."* I can't classify him in any of my categories or psychological states. *"In God, there are neither forms nor images which could be perceived by the memory."* Nothing, then, that corresponds to what I could construct in the human sense. Perhaps I am here in the process of *"walking in the shadows, without seeing any glimmers."* Then, "I trust in the name of the Lord and rely upon him" (see Isa 50:10).

I know that in order to advance, my memory must unite with yours, my God. In order to do this, it must necessarily void itself, empty itself of all of its usual reference points. In any case, they cannot bring one to God. Then, I am called to establish myself in a profound silence, just as my God invited me: "Sit in silence, and go into darkness" (Isa 47:5). That means that I must sit down, and agree to stop for a long time in order to cut off everything that pursues me, everything that preoccupies me, and everything that could make me what I would be except to God. I must do this in silence, not for me to get carried away with memories or to revel in powerless words; in silence, without words, memories, or recollections of any kind—enclosed in the darkness, eyes closed, the imagination under control, the heart waiting to receive love from God, to give it to God.

All of my being is disposed to be completely awaiting you, Lord. All of my being is available, silent, appeased, and removed from all of the invasive upheavals. I listen to you tell me: "Whenever you pray, go into your room and shut the door and pray to your Father who is in secret; and your Father who sees in secret will reward you" (Mt 6:6). It is not from the exterior that I will learn something from you, but in the interior silence of my being, of my heart, when everything in me will be silence. It is not a void, but my control of myself over all that is around me and over what I am, available to my God, void of all creation in order to welcome the bounty of noncreation, whose penetrating presence changes my outlook about people and things. It is your invitation.

Lord, let my memory plunge into your Supreme Good, in a profound lapse of memory, without any memories of anything. For me, this lapse will be an absence or an impossibility. An absence of spontaneous recall, or an impossibility of a reflective recollection or to recall a memory. I don't have to use my energies in order to remind myself. Much more simply, I have to plunge myself into God, by agreeing to lose all of my security mechanisms, all my previous memories. As well, nothing repeats itself. God is always new. If I decide to freeze him in a certain moment that is more savory, he will no longer be there. I will be all alone there with my dreams and memories, without knowing either peace or joy.

The more I become silent, the more I free myself from all of my knowledge, constructions of my intelligence, and the more I empty myself and strip myself of all images, imagination, and illusion, and the more my memory is united to God, the more it aspires to the perfection of the union with God. I will provide a welcome to God who invades my conscience with his eternal and always new presence of love. By emptying myself of everything or agreeing to allow myself to be emptied of everything that is not God, I will become able to *"quench my thirst of the Loved,"* of Jesus, to be *"illuminated by the light he brings to my intelligence.*" Here, my soul *"quenches itself with the memory of the goods it possesses and the delight it has in the union with its Spouse"* (CS, p. 172).

The memory is unique, the one of the Beloved, the memory of the love that he has and that he brings to me, the memory that will abide in me as much as that is possible. The memory of who he is and who calls me to always empty more of myself, to void myself, so that he can invade me even more, penetrating me with his strength of love, making me able to give of myself, making me more desirous of delivering myself to Love. Void of myself in the thirst for God's bounty. It is a state that I can't reach on my own, through my own will, not even through my desire, as pressing as it is. It is a state that could only come from you, Lord, which *"could only be your heart."* I must then always be dispossessed of myself so that you can make the work of your love perfect in me. But, with your help, you want "me to be disposed to the perfection of the union with you. You wait for the time to bless me" (see Isa 30ff).

For my part, I must "wait in silence for the salvation" that comes from you. "Solitary and silent," I wait (see Lam 3:26ff). I wait for the time of your grace, but in the effort to realize a void within me, a silence to establish within me. It must be the silence of everything that is not you, by then accepting *"the negation and deprivation of all forms,"* you progressively dispose me to the union with you; here, you *"put me progressively into the possession of the union with you."* Progressively. You respect who I am, Lord, small as I am compared to your greatness and splendor. You are a penetrating light, but you aren't blinding, so I can welcome you into my life.

And if I am afraid of the void that could be created within me, or of a memory with no recollections, I understand what a bounty you have created within me. *"Since*

God has neither form nor figure, my soul is secure when it divests itself and it then approaches God even more" (VF, p. 202).

This is what echoes within me in this invitation: "Draw near to God and he will draw near to you" (Jas 4:8). To draw myself nearer by keeping *"my memory completely free, without any reflections, neither about the things above nor about the things down below."* My memory must be completely free; without loading it with what I want, what I hear, what I smell and discern, and what I touch. Free, to the point of saving nothing, but *"letting everything fall into a lapse of memory."* Free of everything that could come back spontaneously as in a reflection. Free of everything that could come up into my conscience. Free *"in the lapse of memory of all of creation and everything that is attached to the creatures"* (MC III, p. 59). Free in order to draw nearer to you, Lord, to seize everything in you, to not be possessed by anything and finally, to possess everything in you.

All of my energy is spent not to accumulate memories, but to be free, in order to live of you. Oh, this strips me of everything, for I imagine that the more I accumulate knowledge about you, the more I will fill my memory, the more I will be able to live in you, speak of you, give witness of you. However, it is just the opposite. I must make a void of myself. In your own time, you will make me feel your action within me; when you want to and how you want and never ceasing to hope. Yes, I wait for the time when you will give me the grace, where it will be you who draws near to me in order to take me into you.

REFLECTION QUESTIONS

Am I easily distracted during my day, during the week? Is there a special, quiet place I can go to say my prayers and be with God, listening to him and discerning his will? What assumptions (regarding God, regarding life) do I bring to my prayer time? Can I make an honest attempt to open my heart to the truth of God, despite the fact that it might contradict what I perceive to be the truth?

DAY TWELVE

Purified, I Rest in You

FOCUS POINT

The Lord is always knocking at our door. He is always there, seeking entrance, inviting us to open up to him so that he might transform us, purify us. It is our free will, our "yes," that opens the door to him. We are the Beloved Spouse of God. We are the Mystical Body of Christ. We are God's people, the Church.

> *She* (the soul) lives in solitude.*
> *In solitude, she has her nest;*
> *in solitude she is also guided*
> *alone, by a cherished lover,*
> *he who, very alone as well,*
> *lived of a wounded love.*

---

* John of the Cross refers to the soul as feminine, as if it is the Bride of the Beloved, God. When the soul unites with the Beloved, a Spiritual Marriage is created.

These are the thoughts of the Husband. In this separation from all of creation, where the soul finds itself alone with God, he guides it himself, moves it, and lifts it up to divine things. In other words, its understanding rises all the way to divine intelligence because it is now solitary, disengaged from strange and profane knowledge, its will is freely moved by the love of God, because, up until the present, it was alone and free from all other affections. Its memory fills itself with divine knowledge because it is also solitary, free from the phantoms and fantasies of the imagination....

It is not only said that its Beloved guides it in its solitude, but more than that, that he alone operates within it, with no intermediary. In fact, the very union of a spiritual marriage has this special characteristic: God operates in the soul and communicates himself to it directly through himself and no longer through the actions of the natural faculties. The reason is that all exterior and interior senses, all that is creation and the soul itself, are powerless to contribute to the great supernatural favors that God grants in this state. These favors are in no way within the domain of the natural capacities of the soul, neither a part of its operations, nor a result of its efforts. It is God alone who operates in the soul.

And he does it because he finds it alone. He also permits himself no other company than that of the soul and connects himself with only those things that concern it.

Besides, since the soul has abandoned everything, bypassed all intermediaries, lifted itself towards God by leaving everything else behind, it is righteous that God constitutes its guide himself and makes himself (become) the way which leads it to him. The soul has plunged itself into the void of everything, it has lifted itself above everything; nothing else could help it rise any higher, if it was not the Word himself, its Husband (see CS 35).

In solitude, not alone, for this would be isolation, withdrawal and sadness. But *in solitude* where my only contact is God, and would be God during these days. Like God's chosen people, "I found grace in the wilderness...I seek rest...loved with (God's) everlasting love" (see Jer 31:2, 3). The wilderness and solitude go hand-in-hand. We never cross a wilderness without leaving something of ourselves there, certainly something totally useless, but also a certain thing that we, up until that time, considered to be of the utmost importance. It is a solitude that strips me of myself, which is always cumbersome, and opens me to the God of Love; *"He lives of a wounded love, waiting for the soul who responds to his love."* And on this road, while looking at me, he says to himself: "I will now allure her, and bring her into the wilderness, and speak tenderly to her" (Hos 2:14).

Purified of myself, through my faculties, I am here, available to you, having put aside all of creation, I am here alone with my God. First of all, I am here completely available for him, completely in him: you teach me, Lord, to reach the heights. You lift me all the way to divine things, you put all of my being, all of my faculties into motion, so that all activity, all dynamism comes from you.... You have guided me through the purifying wilderness, not to make me a solitary being, without human surroundings, but to construct me in solitude, face-to-face with you, in full communion with you. In this way, I am completely available for you, you become and you are everything to me. In you, I find all of creation again, but in another way. It is a solitude of abandonment for what I am in order to become a being in communion with what you are. My intelligence, from now on, is purified, lighting the path where you are my only support, Lord, disengaged from everything that is not you and from everything that cannot lead me to you, I am here, resting in you. My will flows with yours, your path becomes mine, it is your love that moves my very fragile will, making it strong. The strength of your love lets me enter into the freedom of your love, rendering my will alone— and it is true that it is I who am acting—and free, with no constraints. Resting in you with a plenitude of being. Even the imagination is appeased.

Memories no longer emerge. My memories are *solitary and free*, totally penetrated by you, Lord, and eager to keep themselves focused on you, preserving what you give me of yourself. You invite me to take "a Sabbath rest" (Heb 4:9), a day blessed with you, Lord, sanctified by you, a day when you contemplate your creative work. You invite me to contemplate, with you, at rest, the work that you accomplished in me during these days. Now, it is a purified love that I give you, in a being that lives for you, *"a love that makes me fly to you, my God, by a solitary path"* (NO, p. 165), a heart-to-heart exchange with you.

It is a heart-to-heart rest that is not inaction, but a profound peace where the Beloved *works alone* in the receptive soul, in his Beloved. It is a heart-to-heart rest to advance even further in the mystery of communion where the Lord calls anyone to let themselves be allured by him: "I will take you for my wife forever…in steadfast love and mercy. I will take you for my wife in faithfulness; and you shall know the Lord" (Hos 2:19, 20). It is for us to listen for this voice from the depths so we can open the door of our heart to God who remains nearby and knocks in order to enter. Our "yes" is awaited. Perhaps if we are profoundly penetrated by the love of God, the God of love will invite himself to the close communion through a "yes" that will be his and ours. "I will come in to you and eat with you, and you with me" (Rev 3:20). It is an alliance between God and the soul, a community of life and love, interpersonal relationship of close communion, a spiritual marriage, if God wants to lead us to this intensity of life. It is a perfect union of love, a total transformation of the Beloved, a reciprocal and mutual gift, where the soul, like God, cannot stop itself.

It is a state that doesn't come from us, but solely from God when he *"communicates himself directly through himself"* to us. Creation can only serve as a springboard to seal this alliance. All of our efforts, even the most generous ones, cannot lead us to this alliance. God *"alone operates within the soul."* *"The spiritual marriage"* which is not reserved only for the wise, the scholarly, the most learned, but to whomever God invites, whoever thirsts for a plenitude of love and lets himself be seized and transformed by him in a capacity to love. A spiritual marriage, the call and response of love which flows from both the heart of God and our heart at the same time because God, in his power of love, has penetrated us with his love.

Everything leaves God in order to descend into our heart and then to return to him, transformed by his own love. "...Those who love me will be loved by my Father, and I will love them and reveal myself to them" (Jn 14:21). It is a manifestation of Jesus, the face-to-face of the Father in love, by giving us his filial capacity to love in order to introduce us into the community of life with the Father of the heavens, in order to live in the alliance. Everything depends upon our capacity to welcome, our capacity to love, and our generosity in love. The more we allow ourselves to be seized by God, the more intense our union with him will be, also the stronger we will be against the Enemy, the one who sows the seeds of disunity. *"When a soul is united to God, the devil fears it as much as God himself"* (ED, p. 212). He can do no serious damage when faced with a soul delivered to God, in one in which God is everything, for which God is everything. That is what we aspire to for perfect communion, for our preferential love, exclusively for God, creation and creatures could be only the springboards that throw us into love. God wants us for himself alone, *"with no other company except his."*

God wants us to be "beings of solitude," before him, gathered in his hands, trusting in his will, which knows what is best for us. God wants us in the state of generous dependency of love, in the radical dispossession of ourselves, in a nothingness that will become everything. *"Oh happy nothingness! Blessed hiding place of the heart, which has the power to bring everything to submit to itself while wanting nothing to submit to it…in order to burn with a more ardent love!"* (ED, p. 289). How could this be if God doesn't dwell in the hiding place of our heart? Without him, we would try to get people and things to submit to us. With him within us, we neither want nor can have things submitted to us. It suffices that we are loved, led by love, led to where we are able to love in this life.

Everything in our life is for God. Ordinary intermediaries are useless; furthermore, they are no longer there. Only God is there. Only God guides us to him and draws us to him. The human ladder has no more rungs for us to climb to reach God, even if that is necessary at the beginning. It is the voiding of nothingness. He is Everything, *"the Word himself, the Husband."* He alone can lift us higher. "Come to me…and I will give you rest" (Mt 11:28); "…abide in my love" (Jn 15:9). Come, stay: a call in the solitude to the only contact with the Beloved. A means of access to the One who is Love and who invites us into the quiet of the community of life and love with him.

REFLECTION QUESTIONS

In what ways is God seeking entrance into my life? If I am truly seeking God in all things, might I make it a point to allow God to speak to me through the various people I encounter throughout my daily life? Am I able to keep an open heart and mind to the possibility that God might reveal his wisdom through the most unlikely of people and situations? Am I humble enough to learn from these unlikely sources?

DAY THIRTEEN

My Gaze Has Become Yours

The Lord sees us first. Eventually, we meet his gaze. The love he gives us is generous and unconditional. It is the deepest, truest love we will ever know. We are transformed by this love, as we seek to give it back to God by sharing it with others. God's love moves us to love.

While you looked at me,
your eyes etched your charms within me,
that is why you loved me out of love;
by that, mine (my eyes) have earned
the right to be able to adore what they see in you.

The distinctive characteristic of perfect love is that it attributes nothing to itself, appropriates nothing for itself, but it sends everything back to the Beloved. If it is like this in human love, what would it be like in the love of God, there, where it is supremely righteous to act in this way?...

"While you looked at me..."

That is to say, while you looked at me with love, for God's gaze is his love.

"Your eyes etched your charms within me..."

Through the eyes of the Husband, it awaits his merciful Divinity, which, bowing with mercy towards a soul, imprints and pours his love and grace into it. This burst communicates a beauty to it, an elevation that makes it a participant in the Divinity itself.

Seeing, then, the dignity and the height to which God has elevated it, it continued:

"That is why you loved me out of love..."

To love out of love is to love profoundly.... When God bestows his grace on a soul, he renders it, through this action, worthy and capable of his love. It is then as if it said: You poured your grace into me; it won your affection for me, that is why you loved me out of love. In other words, that is why you bestowed grace upon me.

Just as God doesn't love anything that is outside of him, in the same way he doesn't love anything with greater strength than himself, because he loves all things for the sake of himself....

For God, loving the soul is to place it in himself, in a certain way, to equalize it with himself. He loves it, then, in himself, with himself, and with the same love with which he loves himself. From there it follows that, by each of its works, if it does it in God, this soul merits the love of its God. I will ex-

plain further: once at this height of grace, by each of its works, it even merits God. It also adds:
          "By that, mine have earned the right..."
That is, by this favor that the eyes of your mercy have granted me while you looked at me and you judged me agreeable to your eyes, worthy of your glance, my own have earned the "right to be able to adore what they see in you" (see CS 32ff).

L ord, your glance is always first, it is a glance of love which comes to make me exist and grow in love. You can't look at me in any other way than by loving me. Am I not the work of your hands? You affirm it to me: "Do not fear, for I have redeemed you; I have called you by name, you are mine...you are precious in my sight, and honored, and I love you..." (Isa 43:1, 4). You love with a gratuitous love. It couldn't be any other way with you. Your eyes etch all sort of things in me, not the things of this world, but those which dwell in you in the depth of your being. You etch in me a part of yourself, that which I am able to welcome. You make me able to read and then able to adore what my eyes see and discover in you. My glance has become your glance, in a community of life and love that you want to experience with me. Your love calls to my love, in the generous gift of myself: by attributing nothing to me of what I am, or what I see, since everything in love is giving; by not appropriating anything for myself of what I give and share, as if it was my work, since everything comes from you, Lord; by sending back to the Beloved the love that he shows me, after having welcomed it into my life. In a way, by returning it to him, he will be completely filled with a life de-livered through love, a life transformed by love, and a life that aspires always to give even more, in a heart completely invaded by the God of love. True love is always a love that grows, but it is also a love to protect. One must be careful to limit one's glance to the exterior of things, to stop one's thoughts about everything that passes and dies. *"All thought that doesn't go to God is a theft for which we will be rendered guilty of to him"* (ED, p. 210). Ignore, then, what is frivolous and useless, everything that distances you from God, everything that distracts you from him. Furthermore, isn't this very thought or glance in each of us a gift from God? "He (God) put the fear of him into their hearts to show them the majesty of his works.... He bestowed knowledge upon them..." (Sir 17:8, 11). If I can see the world through your glance, and if my thoughts, by seizing creation, don't dwell in it, it is because you, Lord, never cease to gaze upon me with your glance, that is, to love me. God's glance is his love. When he fixes his glance on someone, he is giving love (see Mark 10). And the one who is looked upon in this loving way is carried away in the current of God's love by calling upon his own "yes," without constraining his freedom. It is so true that love cannot exist except in reciprocity and truth. But God's love, like the love for God, can only be given to me. It doesn't surge forth from me, but from God, from his husbandly glance, *"from his merciful divinity."* How wonderful it is for me to discover, or rediscover, that our God is not a far off divinity that dominates man and makes him feel his own smallness, crushing him with reproving looks. He is a God of love who looks at me by calling me to love. He is a God with motherly characteristics, full of mercy, *"the God who bows with mercy towards the soul, the God who imprints and pours his love and grace into it."* How one must, through prayer, weigh and seek the depth of meaning of these words with respect to the reality of my life of faith. He is a

God who bows down, and by this, making himself even nearer, putting himself within my reach, so to speak. He is a God who makes an imprint, leaving a mark of what he is, Love. He is a God who pours into me and fills me with his love and all his favors. For God doesn't give something from the exterior to himself. He gives himself, filling my spirit with his own light after having opened it to the aspirations of this light. "He makes the soul pleasing to his eyes" (VF, p. 213) since it is a reflection of God in as much as it is possible for a creature to be. He communicated his beauty to it, the perfect equilibrium of all beings, by lifting him up to the splendors through a participation in the life of God. How wonderful it is to look at myself like this in you, Lord, to perceive what I am in you, in the smallness of my being, lifted up to the dignity, to the heights which permit me, through grace, to keep myself before you. I know that this isn't just a passing moment. You want to fix me in this state of love. "I entered into a covenant with you...and you grew exceedingly beautiful.... Your fame spread among the nations on account of your beauty, for it was perfect because of my splendor that I had bestowed upon you..." (Ezek 16:8, 13, 14). Everything, then, comes from you, Lord. You make me the gift of your love of alliance. You bestow your own splendor upon me. You transform my being through the gift of your grace, by adjusting it to you, by making it a reflection of what you are. But love is always growing, if not, it is no longer love. The more my love for you grows, the more my entire being clothes itself with your own beauty, growing in beauty, ravishing you. And this love that develops is surely your work in me. Through the gift of your grace in me, you make me worthy and able to receive your love. I know it. And there will be days when I will be overflowing with love where my love for you will be so strong that I will believe that everything is possible, but it all comes from you, not me. My experiences bring me back to reality. Enthusiasm is all fine and good, but it doesn't last very long and isn't very faithful. It is a passing thing. I need you to pour your grace into me, for you to spread your love into me. It has never stopped being spread into the world since the day, when you were on the cross, "one of the soldiers pierced your side with a spear, and at once blood and water came out" (Jn 19:34). It was shed for everyone, shed for me so that I welcome your life of love, always drawing from the very wellspring of the cross in the Sacrament of the new Covenant, the supreme gift of your love. It is the Eucharist of the Church, through which you make grace grow within me, you make me conform to your beauty, you flood me with your love, you lift me all the way up to you so that I can always be yours.

In communion with you, I progressively learn to love your way. You love nothing that is outside of you, you love nothing with more strength than yourself because you love all things because you are Love, yourself. Your love for us doesn't separate itself from what you are. If you weren't with me, fulfilling me with your love, I know what would happen to me: I would stop at people and things, love myself in them and not love you in them. You alone can unify my being. You alone can make it so that I love everything in you, and so that nothing separates me from you.

That is it. Since I know and believe that you love me, I understand that puts me in you, that you enclose me in your love, that you love me in your love. I am not exterior to you, Lord, you take me into yourself. *"You love me, then, in yourself, with yourself and with the same love with which you love yourself."* Since I offer thanksgiving for such marvels, I couldn't imagine it if you had not come to reveal them to me in your

Son, your face-to-face of love. Seeing as I am called to a response of love which completely commits me so as to not deceive you! Having reached this life that is emblazed with love, all that I see and all that I do is done in you, for you, as an expression of love. The eyes of your mercy have lifted me all the way to there. Because our gazes are crossed, you make me pleasing to your eyes, you made me worthy to look upon you, you deemed me to merit the ability to see the love in you with which you want to fulfill me. My glance and my heart have become yours by understanding that: *"My Son, I want to give you a Wife who loves you and who, thanks to you, is worthy to keep company with us"* (ED, p. 87). Love calls to love.

REFLECTION QUESTIONS
Besides the love of God for me, who in my life has shown me the greatest example of generous and unconditional love? In what ways did this person model this love? How has that affected the way I love others? When I am filled with God's love, how am I transformed in the way I view other people, especially those with whom I do not always see eye to eye? How might I respond to these people with love?

DAY FOURTEEN

Your Love Always Carries Me Further

FOCUS POINT

Jesus Christ is the center of life and love. The redemption of humanity finds its center in his love. This love he has for us, for me personally, is the motivating force that moves all of us to ever pursue our Lord into greater depths of love. Jesus is the source and summit of love. He provides us with the desire to seek him, offer ourselves to him, seeking full communion with him.

The center of the soul is God. Once it has reached him, according to all of the capacity of its being, according to all the strength of its operation and inclination, it will have reached its last and most profound center, then, with all of its strength, it will love and know God and enjoy him. As long as it hasn't reached this point—as is the case in this mortal life, where the soul can't reach God with all of its powers—it may well be in God, its center, through his grace and the communication he has with it; there is, in it, a movement towards something more, the strength to reach something more, in a way so that it is not satisfied. It is truly in its center, but not in the deepest center, since it could go even further in God.

One must note, in fact, that love is the inclination, strength, and the capacity that the soul possesses in itself to go to God, since it is through the means of love that the soul unites itself with God. The more degrees of love the soul has, the more profoundly it enters into God, and the more it is concentrated on him. Therefore, we could say that the more degrees of God's love the soul reaches, the more centers it reaches in God, each one deeper than the last, for the stronger love is, the more unifying it is....

So for the soul to be in its center, which is God, it suffices for it to have one degree of love, because one degree of love suffices for it to be in God through grace. If it has two degrees of love, it will be centered in God according to another center that is more interior. If it has three degrees, it penetrates into God three times deeper. If it has the last degree, the love of God will wound the soul in its most profound center. In other words, he will transform and enlighten it in all of its being, according to its capacity and strength, until such time as it appears to be God himself. Look at the crystal which is pure and clear. The more degrees of light it receives, the more the light is concentrated in it and the more it shines. And the light could come to be so concentrated in it that it comes to appear to be entirely light, and cannot be distinguished from the light. When it received as much as it is able to receive, it comes to resemble the light itself (VF Commentary, pp. 111, 2:12, 13).

As long as we are on this earth, we continue to love and grow in knowledge and love. Acting like human beings, is to presume to know, that is not to love, since we have enclosed the other forever into a limited dimension of knowledge and love. Since we are speaking of God, who could dare to presume that one could reach the summit of love? In this world, it is impossible. No matter how profound or how elevated our love for God is, it could always be more, with respect to how much we welcome God's gift, which is Love, into ourselves, and with respect to how much God is the center of our soul, of our life. The center is the place where everything converges, the starting point of everything. If the Lord is our center, we owe it to Jesus Christ. "For the love of Christ urges us on...he died for all, so that those who live might live no longer for themselves, but for him who died and was raised for them" (2 Cor 5:14–15). It is thanks to the mystery of Jesus' death and resurrection, the mystery of the Father's love who called for the offering of the Son, the mystery of the Son's love which gave the freely given gift of his life to the Father so that all of his brothers and sisters in humanity would be seized in this redemptive love, that our life discovers its vital center, its luminous point, and hopes to reach it.

God is the center of our entire lives. He draws us to his abyss of love in order to plunge us into it. He wants to lead us to its very depths. Our path towards him then calls for us to live centered upon him with all of the capacity of our being, and with all the strength of our inclination. Everything in us is for him when he will be everything, absolutely everything, for us. Then, *"with all of our strength, we will love and know God and enjoy him."* How good it is to already see the goal, the center from where everything comes and where everything converges. "But then (at the end of the road) we will see

face-to-face. Now I know only in part; then I will know fully"
(1 Cor 13:12). I will know him as fully as I have been known
by him. However, he knew me in his love, an unlimited and
infinite love. He knew me right to the most intimate parts of
myself, my capacities to love, but by injecting all of his love
that I welcomed from him into me there. I will know him as
fully as I have been known by him. That is what motivates me
to go forward all the way to the summit where God waits for
me, for our face-to-face of eternal love. It is a summit that is
always to be reached. It is a summit to reach by twisted roads
which progressively free me from the human environment so
that I can get closer to the light of God. *"To plunge to the very
depths of our center which is God"* (ED, p. 169), or allow
myself to be fascinated by the intense light of the summit, both
are the same. In this world, I have the assurance to be in God;
I know and believe that he is the *"center of my life, the summit"* towards which I am going. I seize how much he communicates himself to me, what gifts of himself he makes to me.
But, just like I will never finish knowing him, I will never finish loving him. I hope to grow in knowledge and love. Lord,
you are the center of my life, but I can't be satisfied with the
stage I am presently at. I hope for the depths of love and the
luminous summit, for *"I am not yet at my most innermost
center."* I perceive, or rather, you made me give birth to a love
that is growing which always takes me further. Love makes me
bow towards you, gives me the strength and ability to progress
towards you. Your love comes to me like many parcels of love
that I welcome throughout the stages. Your love strengthens
me and etches the degrees of love within me that separate me
from the center, the summit. We must push ourselves always
further, always ahead in the degrees of love, in our knowledge
of love, in a way so that we can always enter into God in a

more profound manner, center ourselves more on him. Like
the pebble that we throw into the water that creates concentric circles, this is the way that the love of God produces so
many degrees which, from the further away, bring us back to
the center, to the point of enlightenment, God. From one circle
to the next, we reach out to the center. It takes us from the
degree the furthest away to the closest in order to reach the
center of love, the Living God. The bigger the thing is that is
thrown into the water, the more numerous are the circles it
creates. God is the All who spreads out from an immense number of degrees of love, to the point that he always lives in one
of these circles of love. *"It seems to the soul that the universe
is nothing more than an ocean of love in which it is swallowed
up itself. This love appears to it to be without limits or end"*
(VF, p. 160). But we aspire to the central point, *"for the stronger love is, the more unifying it is."* To God who gives himself,
the soul aspires to give itself, "presented…as a living sacrifice,
holy and acceptable to God" (Rom 12:1), so much so that it
feels carried away by the great current of God's love, the current of an overflowing life. It is a unifying love, a love that
calls for a union with creation, at God's side, so that we will
become able to experience full communion with him.

But it is good for us to hear that all degrees of love, even
the most humble ones, give us a place with God through grace.
That is the first step, the most engaging at times, the one that
will, finally, lead to the second, then the third and all the others. On the path of God's love there is not a predetermined
number of degrees to climb. It is a progression that we must
experience in the light of God. "[T]he true light is already shining. Whoever loves a brother or sister lives in the light" (1 Jn
2:8, 10) of Christ, the light of the world. One who is centered
on the Risen One feels he is overflowing with life and love to

the point of crying out: "[I]t is no longer I who live, but it is Christ who lives in me" (Gal 2:20), the center of love and light, the Life that could no longer withstand any limits, but who aspires for unfailing love, a love that is always growing, all the while knowing that earthly beings will never completely know this intensity.

It is an upheaval for our existence where our love for God will never know bounteous appeasement. It is a dynamism of existence, inhabited by the love of God, with a love that always takes one further. "A disciple is not above the teacher, nor a slave above the master; it is enough for the disciple to be like the teacher…" (Mt 10:24–25). The Master went all of the way to the summit of the cross, a profound upheaval, but it was also a dynamism of a path that finished on the summit of love, in the meeting of two loves, the eternal source of salvation for the world.

There will come a time when *"the love of God will wound the soul in its most profound center."* There will come a time when we will be *"transformed and enlightened in all of our being, according to our capacity and strength, until such time as we appear to be God himself."* We will appear, not be. That is logical about the love of God, since "the one who sanctifies and those who are sanctified all have one Father" (Heb 2:11). Not to come from ourselves, but to appear in the luminous reflection of God until it becomes, through grace, transparent with God.

The crystal is pure, the more it catches the light, the more it gives off. Without light, it is still a crystal, but it doesn't show its richness. It is the same with us. Without God, we show nothing of ourselves. But in the reflection of the love of God that we receive from him, we become completely enlightened, all brilliant with his love, becoming completely like the light, yet without ever being mistaken for it. Transforming love of God, you carry me always further *"until each of us seems to be the other, until you and I make up one single love"* (CS, p. 88). Lord, keep me in the dynamic and exalting mobility of your love.

REFLECTION QUESTIONS

At what moments in my life do I feel the deepest communion with the Lord? During the Mass? In the early morning, as the sun is rising and the day is born anew? In the late evening, as I prepare for sleep, reflecting on the blessings of the day I just experienced? Am I filled with thanks and praise for the Lord's unwavering love for me, for the gifts and graces he gives me throughout my life? How does this generosity affect my relationships with others?

DAY FIFTEEN

Transformed by God, I Find My True Image Again

FOCUS POINT

The Trinitarian relationship is pure love. This love breathes life into humanity, making it possible to love as a reflection of the Trinity. We seek to emulate this perfect love, as we love our fellow human beings, as we love God. The Trinity transforms us by its love, we are drawn in by its breath, by its inspiration, and we share communion with God. (Note: In this context, "inspiration" means the infusion of the breath of the breeze— as in the breathing in of it. Here, inspiration would be the opposite of expiration, breathing out.)

Here is the breath of the breeze.

This "breath of the breeze" is a power that God, the soul as-sures us, will be given to him through communication with the Holy Spirit. Through this divine inspiration (= breathing in), the Holy Spirit lifts the soul up to a sublime height, gives it the necessary information and renders it able to produce, in God, the same inspiration of love that the Father produced in the Son, and the Son in the Father, an inspiration that is the Holy Spirit. In this transformation, the Holy Spirit breathes the soul into the Father and the Son in order to unite them. In fact, if the soul did not transform itself into the three persons of the Holy Trinity in a manifest and evident manner, its transforma-tion would be neither real nor total.

This inspiration of the Holy Spirit into the soul, through which God transforms it, produces delights in it that are so sublime, so exquisite, and so profound that human language is incapable of describing them and human understanding can-not perceive them. Yes, it is impossible to talk about the com-munication that takes place between God and the soul during this transformation here below. In fact, the soul which is united to God and transformed in him even breathes God into God. It is the same divine inspiration through which God inhales, into himself, this soul that has been transformed in him.

Should the soul become capable of an operation as sub-lime as the one that consists of breathing God in, like God breathes it in, through its participation, we should not look upon this as impossible. Given that God deemed it to be united with the Holy Trinity—a union that makes it take on a godlike form and God by participation—is it so incredible that it oper-ates, itself, its work on intelligence, knowledge, and love or, saying it in a better way, that by finding its realization in the Trinity, it operates jointly with this same Trinity? This hap-pens through communication and participation, and it is God

*who operates in the soul. This is precisely what is involved in
the transformation of the three persons, strength, wisdom, and
love. In this, the soul resembles God, and it is as such in order
to bring to him that which had been created in his image and
likeness (see Gen 1:27ff) (CS 39:3, 4).*

L ord, if you have called me to these days of reflection, if you
have placed this strong desire within me to seek you, and
if you let me discover you after having led me on the road of
purification, it is because you hope to give yourself to me in
the most profound manner; it is because you hope to see me
progress to the union of resemblance with you, Lord Jesus; it
is because you want to introduce me into the intimacy of your
life, totally oriented towards the Father, in the dynamic and
personal communion with the Spirit. In his project of love, the
Father "predestined to be conformed to the image of his Son..."
(Rom 8:29). He communicated his Spirit to us, "the Spirit of
God as (adoptive) children of God, the very Spirit that bears
witness...that we are children of God" (see Rom 8:14ff), by
living the life of God, in the image of the Son, transformed by
the Spirit, in such a way that our life is deified. At the heart of
the Holy Trinity, I discover my true image, my true face, thanks
to the action of the Spirit, *"the breath of the breeze,"* that
breeze that is light but also bracing and life-giving. This is what
the Spirit penetrates us with from the depth of love in order to
lift us to a *"sublime height"* where everything is all light and
clarity. Like a true crystal that receives light and shines with all
its fire, we are the same through him, torn away from all of the
impurities of the earth, rendered unable to see anything of what
we are or what we have, totally available and open to the in-

spiration of the love of the Spirit, the light breeze which brings us into his breath of communion and love and makes us be reborn when we have *"a soul that greatly resembles God in purity"* (MC II, p. 112–3). It is the light breeze of the Spirit that inhales us into itself and plunges us into the intimate life of God, the Father, the Source of Life, the Son turned towards the Father, and him, their common Spirit, the gift of Love, their communion to both, in an eternal movement of love which carries us along in praise: "Glory to the Father, through the Son, in the Holy Spirit." The Holy Trinity which wants to introduce us into your life, if it is possible for a created being to commune with you. It is the promise that Jesus made to us: "eternal life...abide in the Father and the Son" (see Jn 5:24), "abide in love" (1 Jn 4:16) "because he has given us of His Spirit" (1 Jn 4:13), "because God's love has been poured into our hearts through the Holy Spirit that has been given to us" (Rom 5:5). I will never fully delve into the significance of these words enough to let their richness fully penetrate my life, like a call to live, like a satiation of this aspiration to live, not only for a certain number of years, but for all time in God's eternity. I will find myself before the Father, when his glance crosses my own, like a Father before his child, a child before his Father, in a face-to-face of love, thanks to the only Son who made me capable of lifting my glance towards the Father, thanks to the Spirit of love who concentrates my glance in such an intensity of love that I could look upon only the Father.

That is my transformation in God, until the union of resemblance with Christ, through the Spirit, for the happiness of the Father. Will I finally understand that God is love? Will I know how to discover his loving face? Will I learn to throw myself into his arms in an act of recognition of his love? By hearing this, perhaps we will be convinced: "The one who loved you, Son, I, myself, have given him, and the love which I have for you, it is the same love I gave him because he had loved the One who I loved so much" (ED, p. 87). These are marvels that can only be experienced in silence, in a state of solitude that is reserved for God alone where we encounter nothing but God, because he is everything, because he is life, because he is love. No one could describe this experience of intense communion to another person, but each of us could remind ourselves of these moments of delights, these sublime times when everything was in God, under the motion of the Spirit, carried away in a powerful spark of love where the senses no longer feel anything, and where the heart can be completely ravished with God. *"The soul which is united to God and transformed in him, even breathes God into God. It is the same divine inspiration through which God inhales, into himself, this soul that has been transformed in him."*

This is an experience of our daily life on earth, at times when God brings himself very close to us and transforms everything in us and around us. They are the delights of our daily life, when in solitude, having placed ourselves alone before God, we find that our outlook on the world has been changed into an outlook of love and praise. It is a radiant peace from the heart, when, plunged into the heart of God, we surpass and withstand the trials of life, because we carry them, thanks to the One who, first, carried his own, not crushed but uplifted by love. It is the happiness of the intelligence and memory that has only one memory, the One of the God of love, the memory whose meaning is fully revealed like an intense call to love. It is an invincible force in the face of obstacles, since the Lord "endowed them with strength like his own, and made them in his own image" (Sir 17:3). The life on earth is already the life of the Kingdom thanks to the Spirit. The soul is engulfed in God. *"It loves, in fact, through the Holy Spirit, just like the Father and Son love each other"* (VF, p. 218), one turned towards the other. In this way, I am called to love, carried by the Spirit, by remaining like a child, my glance fixed upon the Father, whose glance ravishes me, fascinates me and fixes me in his own.

"We are God's children now; what we will be has not yet been revealed. What we do know is this: when he is revealed, we will be like him, for we will see him as he is" (1 Jn 3:2). I have been made for the union of resemblance with my God, today and forever, to live the inspiration of love. "To breathe God in like he breathes me in" is what is necessary, surely "through participation" in it. Just as I am a child of God, through adoption. Through participation, through adoption: that is the reality of life in which God convinces a person to allow himself to be carried along through his own life of love. What a blessing on my road! What acts of thanksgiving must arise from my heart! What loving responses must surge forth throughout my daily life. What new meaning has been given to an existence that is often so humble and dull. What greatness of a life that is entirely lived within the Trinitarian gaze. God deemed to unite me with his Trinitarian life. Through participation, he unites me with what he is, he who only creates and saves through love, for he is Love. I now act in God, I know everything in God, I love in God or, rather, I accomplish everything jointly with the Holy Trinity. It is accomplished without confusion, but through participation and communication in the transformation into the three persons, with the power that comes to me from the Father, the wisdom that the Son shares with me and the love that the Holy Spirit sends to me. *"The soul, becoming the shadow of God, made in God, for God, that which God made in it for himself, and in the*

same manner, of which he made it" (VF, p. 218). Created in
the image and likeness of God, it became *"the shadow of God,"*
the shadow which was produced from his light, a shadow that
would no longer exist without him, a shadow that is tied to
him. I am the image of God, "on which is written a new name"
(Rev 2:17), the name of God. Lord, make me progress on the
earthly path all the way to the perfect union with you, when I
will reach your Kingdom of Glory. Keep me in the breeze of
your Spirit so that my heart will always have the capacity to
love you, You who are Love.

REFLECTION QUESTIONS

How does my understanding of the Trinitarian relationship
affect my relationships with others? If my understanding of
the Trinity is lacking, to what sources might I turn in order to
better understand the mystery of this relationship? Am I aware
of the powerful source of love and grace I invoke each time I
pray the simplest (yet most profound) prayer of the Church,
"in the name of the Father, the Son, and the Holy Spirit"?

Bibliography

To discover more about Saint John of the Cross, the following books are suggested.

Bourne, Peter. *St. John of the Cross: Understanding His Ascent and Dark Night in Easy Stages*. Wenzel Pr., 1995.

Dombrowski, Daniel A. *St. John of the Cross: An Appreciation*. State U. NY Pr., 1992.

Doohan, Leonard. *The Contemporary Challenge of John of the Cross: An Introduction to His Life and Teaching*. ICS Pubns., 1995.

Frost, Bede. *St. John of the Cross: Doctor of Divine Love, an Introduction to His Philosophy, Theology, and Spirituality*. Gordon Pr., 1977.

Kinn, James W. *Contemplation 2000: St. John of the Cross for Today*. St. Bedes Pubns., 1996.

Lyddon, Eileen. *Door Through Darkness: John of the Cross and Mysticism in Everyday Life*. New City Pr., 1995.

Muto, Susan A. and Van Kaam, Adrian. *Words of Wisdom for Our World: The Precautions and Counsels of St. John of the Cross*. ICS Pubns., 1996.

Muto, Susan. *Dear Master: Letters on Spiritual Direction Inspired by St. John of the Cross*. Liguori/Triumph, 1999.

Simsic, Wayne. *Praying with John of the Cross*. Koch, Carl,
    ed. St. Mary's Pr., 1993.
Welch, John W. *When Gods Die: An Introduction to St. John
    of the Cross*. Paulist Pr., 1990.